Praise for *Rewilding*

"Climb a tree, roll in the grass, wander in the woods. *Rewilding* is a reflection, an invitation, a poem, a reminder that reawakens our senses."

JACK KORNFIELD, PHD
author of *A Path with Heart*

"*Rewilding* is packed with beautiful information and practices to take you straight to the beating heart of true enlightenment—a willingness to be with Nature as it is, as our greatest teacher. Truly, Micah's book represents the next generation of authentic spiritual inquiry—a space where the wildness of communion with Nature can coexist with the etheric realms of our human heart. This book is a great gift to anyone interested in a transformational journey that brings us down into the roots of who we are and where we come from. I can't wait to start reclaiming my ancient skills."

KATIE SILCOX
New York Times bestselling author
of *Healthy Happy Sexy: Ayurveda
Wisdom for Modern Women*

"*Rewilding* addresses perhaps one of the most urgent issues of our time—a global nature deficiency disorder that is linked to a host of health concerns, including imbalances found in Nobel Prize-winning science on our circadian rhythms. This is must-read!"

JOHN DOUILLARD, DC, CAP
bestselling author and founder of LifeSpa.com

"*Rewilding* reads as easily as a mountain stream—go ahead, open any page and notice how you feel."

GORDON HEMPTON
author of *One Square Inch of
Silence* and founding partner
of Quiet Parks International

"With tenderness and insight, Micah Mortali leads us in ways to reconnect with our living earth. *Rewilding* is an essential first step to restoring our souls—so we can, in turn, restore our sweet, green, broken world before it's too late."   SY MONTGOMERY
author of the *New York Times*
bestseller *How to Be a Good Creature:
A Memoir in Thirteen Animals*

"Through this inspiring and insightful book, Micah Mortali reminds us of the importance of connecting to the earth and the surrounding environment as a teacher of deep meditative wisdom, as well as for health and well-being. The reader is invited to re-discover that they are part of the cycles and dynamism of life. This recognition of our inherent relationship to the world is particularly relevant today as we have begun to learn both the adverse health effects of isolation and the healing benefit of connection—particularly to our environment."

MARLYSA SULLIVAN, PT, C-IAYT
assistant professor, Maryland University
of Integrative Health

REWILDING

MICAH MORTALI

REWILDING

MEDITATIONS, PRACTICES, AND SKILLS
FOR AWAKENING IN NATURE

FOREWORD BY STEPHEN COPE

sounds true
BOULDER, COLORADO

Sounds True
Boulder, CO 80306

This book is not intended as a substitute for the medical recommendations of
physicians, mental health professionals, or other health-care providers. Rather, it is
intended to offer information to help the reader cooperate with physicians, mental
health professionals, and health-care providers in a mutual quest for optimal well-
being. We advise readers to carefully review and understand the ideas presented
and to seek the advice of a qualified professional before attempting to use them.

Published 2019

Cover design by Jennifer Miles
Book design by Beth Skelley
Illustrations © 2019 Meredith March

Printed in Canada

Library of Congress Cataloging-in-Publication Data

Names: Mortali, Micah, author.
Title: Rewilding : meditations, practices, and skills for awakening in nature /
  Micah Mortali ; foreword by Stephen Cope.
Description: Boulder, CO : Sounds True, [2019] | Includes bibliographical
  references and index.
Identifiers: LCCN 2019010436 (print) | LCCN 2019012781 (ebook) |
  ISBN 9781683644224 (ebook) | ISBN 9781683643258 (pbk.)
Subjects: LCSH: Nature--Psychological aspects. | Nature—Religious aspects. |
  Nature observation. | Mindfulness (Psychology)
Classification: LCC BF353.5.N37 (ebook) | LCC BF353.5.N37 M67 2019 (print) |
  DDC 155.9/1—dc23
LC record available at https://lccn.loc.gov/2019010436

10 9 8 7 6 5 4 3 2 1

This book is dedicated to Solia, Stryder, Cora, and the children of 2229: our seventh generation. Each generation has its seventh generation to look out for. They are ours.

In gratitude to the Haudenosaunee Confederacy for the wisdom to think of those yet to come when making decisions.

Special thanks to my parents, who helped to awaken and nurture my relationship with the earth.

DEEP ROOTS ARE NOT REACHED BY THE FROST.

J. R. R. TOLKIEN

CONTENTS

FOREWORD

During the fall and winter of 1850 and 1851, Henry David Thoreau, America's great philosopher and naturalist, was deeply immersed in an investigation of his growing experience of what he would call "The Wild." He had come to believe that the very energy and genius of humankind was to be found only in a deep, mystical connection with our own inner "wildness." "Life consists with wildness," he wrote in his oft-delivered lecture entitled "The Wild," first given live to an audience in 1851. "The most alive is the wildest. . . . All good things are wild and free."

But what is this wildness that Thoreau seeks out and longs for? Do we long for it as well? You have in your hands a book entitled *Rewilding*. Does this mean that you feel, as Thoreau did, some lack of wildness in your life?

Keep in mind that Thoreau was a profoundly civilized man. Only a decade before his great affair with wildness, he had graduated from Harvard University—a place we might think of as decidedly "unwild"—where he excelled in Latin and Greek, in the study of the classics, in philosophy and ancient history, and a multitude of modern languages. He was devoted to knowledge. To the highest in Western civilization. To the wisdom of the great human cultures.

But had he somehow in his vast educational journey missed a connection with his inner ape?

Yes, he had. By his midthirties, Thoreau had come to believe that the journey to the highest pinnacle of human knowledge must lead beyond all of the book learning he had mastered. It must lead inexorably to a deep reacquaintance with the natural world from which we spring. In midlife, he fairly explodes with rapture in his discovery of the sublime in nature. His writing pulsates with these discoveries. In what he calls his "newer testament," he calls for a great awakening to nature—to The Wild. He sings out his credo: "I believe in the forest, and in the meadow, and in the night in which the corn grows."

Can we identify with Thoreau in his search for the missing parts of human experience? Yes, of course we can. It is useful for us to remember that by the mid-1850s, visionaries such as Thoreau were already perceiving a profound deficit in our modern ways of living—were already seeing how we had lost our connection with the natural world. Their proclamations were, of course, an early identification of what we now call "nature deficit disorder."

But Thoreau anticipated us in more ways than this. In addition to being one of our greatest naturalists, he was, famously, one of the first American proponents of the study of Eastern religion, and, perhaps especially, of the yoga tradition. Indeed, the great yogic scripture called the Bhagavad Gita was one of the few books Thoreau always had at his side during his two-year pilgrimage at Walden Pond. "Even I," he wrote, as he sat on the edge of the pond at first morning light, "am a yogi!"

Thoreau's journey to Walden Pond was an outward and visible sign of his return to his deepest self, and he associated this journey home with his study of the Eastern classics. He identified himself with what yogis call "the quest for the fully alive human being," or in Sanskrit, the *jivan mukti*. He would certainly have known that one of the very highest stages in the development of the fully alive human being is the recognition that "all living beings are made of the same stuff." (That is exactly how the yoga scriptures word it: "the same stuff.") He would have known that all of those beings in the forest and the meadow and the cornfield were made of exactly the same stuff from which he was made. He would have understood that *in knowing them, he knew himself more deeply*. He would have seen himself as part of the family of nature.

In this brilliant new book, Micah Mortali stands on the shoulders of Thoreau in so many ways, bringing our quest for wildness into the twenty-first century. He acknowledges our longing for this lost part of our oh-so-civilized selves. And then more: he gives us simple, useful, and elegant practices through which we can reclaim this lost part.

In Thoreau, every exterior journey—the journey into the meadow and the forest and the cornfield—is also a journey into the beautiful internal world of the human mind, the human imagination, the human soul. What is outside is inside. And what is inside is outside. And the highest stage of this homecoming in the yoga tradition is called *samadhi*, which literally means "bringing the world together."

Micah Mortali writes in the highest tradition of both Thoreau and yoga, from which he himself springs. His book, indeed, "brings the world together." The interior and the exterior. The civilized and the uncivilized. The human and the more-than-human. We are grateful for this wonderful effort.

Stephen Cope
Scholar Emeritus
Kripalu Center for Yoga & Health

INTRODUCTION

Rewilding is a coming home to our roots. It is a recognition that this planet and our local environments are priceless gifts from the forces of life in our universe. To rewild is to reach out and embrace the earth. The concept of wildness, like Tarzan, is the invention of a society at odds with nature. Rewilding is a return to our essential nature. It is an attempt to reclaim something of what we were before we used words like "civilized" to define ourselves.

We live in a time when technology dominates our lives. The internet and portable touch-screen devices have radically altered our interactions and our societies. Fewer and fewer people are connected to the source of their food or the land on which they live. This break in our relationship to nature alienates us from the generative forces of our living earth and may alienate future generations, with catastrophic consequences. Indeed, it seems apparent now that effects of this disconnection are already happening around the world.

We evolved in intimate contact with the land, the seasons, and what author David Abram calls "the more-than-human world," a term I use for nature. Rewilding reacquaints us with our environment and ourselves. It draws us out to experience the comfort and joy of a sacred fire, the sweetness of a freshly picked wild berry, the interspecies connection we make when we come eye to eye with a wild creature, and the fellowship of friends sitting on the earth sharing stories of their day.

Rewilding calls us from our indoor environments and virtual worlds and asks us to adapt to the real world, the natural world. It helps us recover and enliven our senses, which may have been dulled by the monotony of indoor environments. By stepping outdoors, lifting our noses to the sky, smelling the wind, taking a long view, and becoming students of nature, we can learn to respond skillfully to the real-life conditions on our home planet—for the seasons on our planet and the relative equilibrium of our climate are rapidly changing, and in order to face this, we need our senses about us, we need to be aware and alert, and we need to know basic skills to help us discern the wisdom of nature and stay close to it.

As a child, I spent a lot of time outdoors. My parents and I lived off the grid for about a year while they built our house in the woods. We heated with wood, pumped water from a well, and used candles and kerosene lanterns for our evening illumination. That experience had a deep and lasting impact on me, and as I grew, getting outside and being close to the elements was of prime importance. Nature was my medicine and my solace and inspiration through trying times as a child, after my parents' divorce, and during the turbulence of my adolescence and young adulthood. I feel very fortunate to have grown up close to the land, wandering through woods and fields unsupervised. Using my bow and arrows to shoot at cans and stumps, climbing trees, making fires, and building forts provided a sense of adventure and helped me grow in confidence. Growing up close to the land also led me to appreciate the simple beauty and profound mystery of the natural world.

Time outdoors nourishes both our contemplative and adventurous sides. As a kid, I moved between pretending that I was in *The Lord of the Rings* or *Robin Hood* to pausing in the woods and being totally swept up by the sound of the wind in the birches. I pondered the great questions: Who am I? What am I? How did we all get here? On a quiet afternoon, a small, crackling fire on top of the old "bear cave" in the forest behind my dad's house was profoundly moving to my soul. It affected me more than any sermon I ever heard in church on Sunday morning. The smell of burning dry pine branches and the occasional pop of exploding sap guided me into a natural state of present-moment awareness and powerful communion with my senses and the living earth. Yet what was normal life in the woods for me, I realized many years later, was foreign and strange for other people who grew up with cable TV and video games. Outdoor pursuits made me feel alive and connected, and the skills I developed seemed to invite a natural state of mindful reverie.

As I grew up (slowly), I vacillated between feeding my hunger for the outdoors and following my interest in spirituality and mysticism, which led me to study religion and eventually to explore the worlds of yoga and meditation. I have been practicing yoga now for over twenty years, and guiding others outdoors for just as long. I've been a Kripalu Yoga teacher; a mindful volunteer dishwasher (a profound learning experience); a therapeutic wilderness counselor with at-risk teens; an outdoor educator for middle schoolers; a yoga retreat leader; a residential volunteer manager; a student of ancestral skills; a director of the Kripalu Schools of Yoga, Ayurveda, and Integrative Yoga Therapy; and most recently a founder and lead trainer of mindful outdoor guides in the Kripalu School of Mindful Outdoor Leadership. My work, which has evolved into supporting change agents through the many trainings and programs that we run at the Kripalu Center for Yoga & Health, our nation's largest yoga-based retreat center, has allowed me to express and communicate my passion for mindfulness and rewilding practices in exciting ways.

I approach the practice of human rewilding through the lens of mindfulness, which I sometimes define as "nonjudgmental, present-moment awareness," as well as through the philosophies, methodologies, and practices of yoga. In the pages ahead, I present meditations and other practices for rewilding that will usher you into a new—or renewed—relationship with nature and help you grow in self-understanding. Being outside and exploring the natural world support a calm and alert state of mind—and learning to deepen and stabilize that state through breathing practices, meditation, and other techniques that connect you with nature can make your experience even more rewarding.

As my own calling to pursue this path took shape, the need for this important work was building across the world. Disconnection from self, community, and nature is increasing, as are depression, anxiety, and other mental health challenges. Average Americans are now on screens for eleven hours a day, according to a Nielsen study, and spend 90 percent of their lives indoors, according to a study by the Environmental Protection Agency.[1] The crises in our global environment, from climate change and species loss to plastic garbage gyres in the world's oceans and conflicts over resources, are accelerating. Rewilding can't solve all these issues quickly, but I believe it can help to support a reconnection between people and the living earth. Part of this reconnection is a remembering of what is important and essential: clean air and water, healthy ecosystems and healthful food, shelter and community.

Rewilding can help you to take a deep breath, walk with your feet on the ground, and sit by a fire as you listen to the wind in the trees. It can help you settle back into a wisdom that is older than language and written history, something foundational to who you are. It can help us all remember what we are, where we belong, and how much we have to be grateful for on this precious planet, for the seasons still turn and birds still sing in the trees. Anyone can take a few minutes to breathe, to learn who we share this land with, and to become a part of our forests and wild communities again. We just need to slow down and open our senses to the wonder that is all around us.

A ditch somewhere—or a creek, meadow, woodlot, or marsh . . . These are places of initiation, where the borders between ourselves and other creatures break down, where the earth gets under our nails and a sense of place gets under our skin . . . Everybody has a ditch, or ought to. For only the ditches—and the fields, the woods, the ravines—can teach us to care enough for all the land.

Robert Michael Pyle, *The Thunder Tree*

1
MINDFUL REWILDING

When I lead outdoor programs and retreats, I often invite partici-
pants to remove their shoes for periods of slow, mindful walking in
nature. One beautiful trail I like to use runs along a stream where
the ground is smooth and easy on the feet, especially for those who
don't have calluses from years of going barefoot. I invite everyone to
close their eyes and slow their breathing. We feel the sensation of our
feet touching the earth, and as we begin to walk, we stay connected
to our breathing. We move without any talking or social interaction.
A five-hundred-yard stretch of trail can take thirty minutes to cover
at our mindful pace. We are unhurried, in the moment. You can try
this yourself in your own neighborhood or home, and take as long
as you like.

Afterward, we gather back together as a group, sit in a circle, and
pass a stone around from one person to another. Whoever holds the
stone has the authority to speak, and everyone else listens with compassion to the speaker's observations and experience. What I hear them
say time and again is that they have not walked barefoot on the earth
for ten, fifteen, or even more years. After one group walked barefoot
across an expansive lawn toward a tree they had chosen, one participant said that he found it difficult to maintain his balance without

shoes, that he had almost fallen over three or four times. It had been twenty-five years, he said, since he had walked barefoot on grass.

The simple practice of walking barefoot on the earth and bringing awareness to the sensual experience of contact and connection can be life changing. It's about so much more than just being barefoot. It's about opening yourself to sensual contact and relationship with nature. It's about a willingness to feel and connect with the great web of life that surrounds us, penetrates us, and binds us all together.

Making physical contact with the earth through the senses is one of the pillars of human rewilding. Another is connecting to where our food comes from and participating in its procurement. Whether you forage for wild berries or grow tomatoes, dig for clams in a tidal flat or at the edge of the surf, fly-fish for trout or bow-hunt for whitetail deer, rewilding is about reestablishing a connection to your place in the food chain and to the other living things that sustain our lives.

Rewilding is actually a vast subject, and it can pertain to the rewilding of ecosystems by reintroducing species that were extinguished, such as wolves or bobcats, or to the rewilding of human life by exploring ways of connecting with the earth and living more in harmony with it. Some people focus on wilderness survival, while others geek out on natural or primal movement patterns for the body, exploring how to go barefoot and move gracefully and powerfully over the land. Others are drawn to ancestral skills, such as friction fire-making, shelter building, animal tracking, or flint knapping to make ancestral tools. Still others explore plant medicine, foraging, wild food harvesting, or shamanic healing practices. Any one of these subjects could take up an entire book, but I'll keep our focus on personal rewilding, or the practice of mindfulness in nature, which connects us to our original natural or wild essence.

At one time across the continents, all of our ancestors lived close to the earth, its seasons, cycles, and many life-forms. Today, many people in the developed world are far removed from contact with nature and living lives of constant stress. Most people today recognize more corporate logos than the flora and fauna in their bioregion. Modern environments are often "ecologically boring," as environmental activist and journalist George Monbiot writes, and do not refresh the mind or support the health of the nervous system.[1] Think about the average office environment or chain store, with its fluorescent lights, few windows, stale air, and computer screens. These places dull our senses, and their sterility can make us sick. Health crises that arise from sedentary lifestyles have increased dramatically around the world, and these diseases track closely with the disruption and destruction of our climates and planet.

Perhaps separating people from the earth is a purposeful effort by modern companies and governments. For the further we individuals are from intimately knowing our lands, the easier it is for organizations to destroy environments and the clean air and water on which we depend, in the name of progress and economic growth. With so many people spending so little time establishing healthy bonds with nature, who will speak for the planet? Where will the future earth stewards come from?

Rewilding offers a way out of this unsustainable cycle of existence, and it gives us a variety of ways to live in closer relationship with the earth, which also allows us to live in deeper relationship to the self. Our bodies, senses, minds, and hearts are but one expression of one species, one manifestation of the living earth. When we draw closer to the field of life pulsing through our feet, flowing through our lungs, and moving through our digestive tract, we are communing with a larger, more expansive model of who and what we are. In this sense, rewilding is also a journey of self-realization that leads us into nature, both the natural world we find within ourselves in deep meditation and the natural world we find in the forests, oceans, fields, and mountains of this living earth. In either case, it is a journey of self-discovery.

The great historian and theologian Thomas Berry put it this way:

> In ourselves the universe is revealed to itself as we are
> revealed in the universe. Such a statement could be made
> about any aspect of the universe because every being in the
> universe articulates some special quality of the universe
> in its entirety. Indeed, nothing in the universe could be
> itself apart from every other being in the universe, nor
> could any moment of the universe story exist apart from
> all of the other moments in the story. Yet it is within our

own being that we have our own unique experience of the universe and of the Earth in its full reality.[2]

Rewilding is an endeavor to be awake, alive, and aware on a planet that is crying out for us to listen and respond with skill and wisdom. It is a journey of coming home to our human selves, to a reunion with our sensing and feeling animal bodies. In rewilding we awaken to the miracle of life, give thanks for every breath, and assume our role as caretakers of this precious and sacred living earth. We remove the shoes that insulate us from the energy flowing in the grass and through the earth and stones. We open our windows and listen to the language of birds, wind, and clouds; the voices of thunder, rain and space; and the sounds of the moon and the stars.

Ecological and Human Rewilding

> Man always kills the things he loves, and so we the pioneers have killed our wilderness. Some say we had to. Be that as it may, I am glad I shall never be young without wild country to be young in. Of what avail are forty freedoms without a blank spot on the map.   **ALDO LEOPOLD**

For hundreds of thousands of years, our species lived intimately with the earth. We were in the wild and of the wild. Efforts to rewild ecosystems aim to protect lands from human development, creating wildlife corridors that allow animals to move from one area to another and reintroducing keystone species or apex predators, whose presence is essential for the overall health of the ecosystem in which they evolved. When these animals are absent, imbalances occur. For instance, white-tail deer populations now overpopulate suburbs around the country because natural predators are lacking. This leads to a variety of negative ecological impacts, such as soil erosion and the destruction of plant species on which other animals depend; the loss of native species, including birds; and the overgrowth of nonnative species. It also results in sickness and starvation of the deer themselves.

Internationally respected environmentalist Bill McKibben has proposed that half of the earth's land and water be set aside as wild in order to minimize humankind's negative effects on the planet's systems. In such a model, rewilded ecosystems would only require minimal human management because they would in essence regulate themselves with a natural balance of predator and prey. The intelligence of the living earth would be in charge, as it was before humans became such a dominating force.

Other proponents of rewilding ecosystems advocate for the reintroduction of apex predators, such as mountain lions in North America, wolves in Scotland, and even elephants in Europe. Apex predators could not only help restore ecological balance but also contribute to the psychological well-being of the people who live near them. In his book *Feral*, George Monbiot writes about an interesting phenomenon: people all over Great Britain frequently report seeing wild large cats. These sightings of ABCs (Alien or Anomalous Big Cats) number well over a thousand, and the authorities have thoroughly investigated every report—though no large cats have been found to exist or to breed there. Monbiot posits that humans have an innate need to be in relationship with large predators, that their existence is inextricably bound with our own. Without them, we feel a sense of emptiness and loss.[3]

This psychological need for the presence of large animals, especially cats, historically our most feared predator, is deep and may lead to the large volume of false sightings. Perhaps this is similar to the phantom pain that a person missing a limb experiences (when the brain produces pain in neurons that correspond to a limb that is absent). Perhaps our minds produce phantom images of a vanished member of our natural world. Harvard biologist E. O. Wilson refers to humankind's fascination and need for interaction with other life-forms as "biophilia," while Native American scientist and professor of environmental biology Robin Wall Kimmerer refers to our modern disconnection from other life-forms as "species loneliness."[4]

> To the degree that we come to understand other
> organisms, we will place a greater value on them,
> and on ourselves. E. O. WILSON[5]

Recently, while walking out my backdoor one morning to see what new animal tracks I might find, I noticed that the goldenrod growing along my border with the woods was trampled in a big circular path. The trail, which had been thoroughly compressed, led to a patch of black raspberries. It was clear that a black bear had been here very recently and that the bear had enjoyed a meal. In fact, I had been out there just an hour before and not noticed the trail, so the bear may have been by just moments ago. When I came back out, I had my daughter Cora with me and showed her the bear trail. Her eyes went wide. It's exciting to live so close to such animals. The week prior, while I was sipping my coffee and listening to the morning chorus of birds, a large bobcat crossed the backyard and headed into the forest. The furious alarms from jays and robins followed that cat into the woods and beyond. What a gift it is to share the land with such beautiful and powerful beings!

Living in the hills of western Massachusetts, I feel fortunate to have black bears, coyotes, bobcats, and even the occasional mountain lion pass through. Spending time alone in the deep woods and knowing that these creatures also share this land awakens a great hope in me. I grew up in Connecticut before the return of the wild turkey and the emergence of the eastern coyote, and when there weren't any bears around. As a young man in those woods, I longed for some greater encounter, even a taste of danger, more than what the deer and ticks could afford me. Just knowing that these powerful creatures are here now sharpens my senses. I am more alert and aware. I know that these other beings are not out to get me, of course, but I also know that they are faster and stronger than I.

Off the coast of Cape Cod, in Massachusetts, seals have returned to the waters, and they've been followed by great white sharks who come to feed on them. Over the past few years, during our family trips to the Cape, I have noticed that these powerful predators shape how I feel in the water. As with the bears and the large cats near my home, I know that I am back on the food chain when I see seals swimming just ten to twenty feet offshore because I know that the great whites are hunting nearby, however unlikely an attack is.

In the Berkshires, people love talking about bears, bobcats, mountain lions, coyotes, fishers, and other wild predators that live in the region. Like Monbiot, I wonder if this fascination is a longing for connection with the alpha predators that held such an important role in our lives for hundreds of thousands of years. The bear and the wolf are mega-entities in the human psyche. Some anthropologists believe that the earliest evidence of human religious behavior was the worship of the cave bear *(Ursus spelaeus)*, whose remains have been found in the Chauvet Cave in France, along with magnificent red paintings of these enormous bears. These creatures were the gods of old. They were the teachers, spirits, and ancient dangers of a world before humans developed written language.

When guests come to my retreats at Kripalu and see signs that advise them to be aware of bears, their eyes widen, as my daughter's did, and they smile. They enjoy the sense of adventure that a wild animal's presence brings, the idea that they are somewhere where bears roam and that they might encounter one on a trail. This is primal stuff. The fascination with which people respond to the presence of our wild friends speaks to our loneliness as a species and our need for connection with the more-than-human world.

My barber is a local man who lives on the other side of my mountain. He often shares with me reports about a black bear who lives in our woods. According to him, when the bear stands on its hind legs, a white patch of fur in the shape of a heart is visible on its chest. He calls the bear "White Heart" and says the creature is old, large, and legendary. I've never seen White Heart, but I love the story. One day I hope to see him standing in the goldenrod, eating black raspberries. What I love about White Heart is that the bear is a local legend on our little mountain. Once upon a time, every forest, mountain, and little hamlet had its own legends. I hope rewilding will give that to us again.

Sightings of mountain lions have also long been reported in western Massachusetts. The state says that there is no evidence that mountain lions are breeding here, but if they're not living here, they certainly seem to be passing through. One mountain lion that was killed by a car in Connecticut in 2011 had traveled 1,500 miles. And according to my barber, a hunter friend had the following experience.

While sitting in his tree stand one October during hunting season, the hunter got the funny feeling that he was being watched. He turned to look behind him but saw nothing. When he lifted his gaze to follow the trunk of a white pine up above his position, there in the crook of the tree, thirty-five feet off the ground and fifteen feet above him, he saw the body of a dead deer! What animal is strong enough to carry a dead deer thirty-five feet up a tree? There's only one: a mountain lion.

When my barber told me this story, I got a chill, as I would from a science-fiction or horror movie. Is this story true? It certainly could be, and I can imagine how humbling it would be to see something like that. It was an indication for that hunter that he was definitely not the only predator in those woods.

Modern life shields many of us from those kinds of experiences, though you certainly don't need to be a hunter to draw closer to the cycles of predator and prey. You need only to make a habit of sitting outside in a regular spot to watch the birds. Before long, a whole other world will begin to open. We'll explore some practices for peaceful encounters with nature and our relatives later on in the book.

Domestication Antidote

Modern people have become domesticated. We trade a part of our essential wildness to be part of society. We trade our time at jobs for food, shelter, and the other essentials we need for survival. The term *domestication* comes from the Latin word *domesticus*, which means "belonging to the house." Considering our modern, sedentary, and indoor lifestyle, "belonging to the house" seems an accurate description of most people's lives today. In creating safety, creating places without edges, without danger, without risk, we have removed the element of gravity, the downward pressure that strengthens bones, muscles, and will. Domestication has brought us comforts, but not a sense of accomplishment, gratitude, or humility.

With personal rewilding, we relearn ways of being in relationship to the earth, ways that predate the agricultural and industrial revolutions. Making a fire or a shelter is not just done for utility; it can be a work of art, a reverent expression of our love for the gifts of life. World-renowned founder of the Tracker School, in the Pine Barrens of New Jersey, Tom Brown Jr. learned from his teacher Stalking Wolf, an Apache tracker, that ancient skills were always taught with thanksgiving and reverence for the living earth.

Acquiring and using these skills is profoundly transformational. The bow drill, for example, involves birthing fire by creating friction. You use a small bow that turns a spindle on a hearthboard to create smoke and eventually a small coal that, if handled carefully and attentively, can be breathed into fire in the palm of your hand. When I demonstrate this technique, people are often brought to tears. There is something primal, ancient, and profound about taking part in this ceremony. Before people experience it, however, they often ask me, "Why do you need to know how to make fire with a bow drill?" It's as if they think that because we have matches now, there is no value in knowing the old ways. I can't blame them for asking, since they have never experienced what it is like to embody the archetype of Prometheus and bring forth the element of fire through sweat, focus, dedication, and surrender of the ego. It changes you.

Are we different from our wild ancestors who lived outdoors year-round and hunted, gathered, or grew their food in relationship with the seasons and the living earth? And if we have changed, can we rediscover and reignite our essential wildness and intimacy with nature's forces?

I believe we can, and I'm eager to share with you the methods and practices I promote to rewild my students. First, let's explore a little about the effects of domestication on us and why we would want to supplement our "sivilizing" (as Huck Finn spelled it) with rewilding.

Nonuke the Wild

When I was five years old, my parents adopted a Siberian Husky and named her Nonuke, a take on *Nanook of the North*, the 1922 documentary about the Inuit people, and also a nod to my parents' role in the antinuclear-power movement following the accident at the Three

Mile Island power plant. As a little boy, I was thrilled to finally get a dog. I imagined her sleeping on my bed and being a loyal and loving companion. When we brought her home, I asked if I could walk her. But when my dad handed me her leash, she took off running so hard and fast that I was literally dragged down the gravel road on my chest for fifteen feet. Cut, scraped, and crying, I was astonished by her raw pulling power and saddened that she wasn't the docile companion I had hoped she would be.

Nonuke went on to break every rope and lead we ever put on her. No matter how we tried to train her and keep her home, she always escaped. Once she jumped out of my dad's Jeep on the highway, and another time when she was loose, she attacked a poodle that walked in front of her mate's house. One Saturday, she returned to us after being gone for days, bounding out of the woods with a deer leg in her mouth, as happy as I ever saw her. Whenever it snowed, she was in ecstasy. Once when we were out in the snow, she ran at me so hard from behind that she flipped me up and onto my back before I even knew she was coming. Then she turned toward me with her big tongue hanging out and her eyes smiling, so perfectly in her element. She was a husky, and huskies need to run. Nonuke couldn't live on a leash, in a crate, or in an apartment. It wasn't in her nature, and she never surrendered. She always broke free and expressed her wildness—no matter what.

Like many people today, I often wish I didn't need to drive a car at all. Although I love my work and must travel to my workplace, I often feel trapped in my modern lifestyle. With a mortgage, grocery bills, and all of the other aspects of life that require money, I feel compelled to stay on the hamster wheel, even though I know I am contributing to the degradation of the earth. Sometimes, in meetings at work or sitting in a chair for hours at a time, I feel cooped up and jittery. I want to stand up and move. I watch my coworkers chewing gum, clicking their pens compulsively, adjusting their papers, rearranging their folders, and moving their phones from here to there and back again. I can feel their urge to move, and I know the self-control required to sublimate these ancient impulses. I look out the window and feel the way I did in second grade, counting down the minutes to recess or the end of the day, the time when I could kick off my shoes and climb a tree. Nonuke wouldn't sit still. She would break free.

We can all learn how to break free, a little at a time, in spirit, mind, and body. First, though, we will identify what we're missing so that we can restore what we need.

Reversing Ecological Boredom

George Monbiot coined the term "ecological boredom" after he had lived in the field as a journalist for years, covering the wild and dangerous gold boom in the rainforests of Brazil.[6] After he returned home to Great Britain to live in suburbia, with a lawn to mow and a dishwasher to empty, Monbiot found that something important was missing, something he had discovered in Brazil. Back in the safe and predictable developed world, he missed the experience of sleeping outside in the rainforest, in spite of the danger of bandits. He also missed the day-to-day struggle to survive. He missed the sense of being alive that he experienced in the wild, a feeling that did not follow him home.

I sometimes call this ecological boredom "life-force deficit." It's a loss of sensory stimulation from the ecosystems and life-forms that our nervous systems evolved with. Addressing this loss is part of the impetus for human rewilding. Sitting at a desk, staring at a computer, being inside an office, cut off from sunlight, fresh air, and the sounds of nature, we live an indoor life, a life of the house. I am reminded of Theodore Roszak's book *The Voice of the Earth*, in which he talks about the dramatic change in the human environment, from the sensory rich and diverse outdoors that our hunter-gatherer ancestors experienced every day to the sensory dull and limited indoors we now inhabit. This makes us prone not only to lifestyle diseases (obesity, heart disease, and diabetes, among many others) but also to increased psychological disorders.

In many societies, we are expected and encouraged to consume products for the health of the economy, aiming for infinite growth. As a result, we find ourselves cut off from the earth, which is deemed a resource rather than the source of our lives. I believe the shift needed in our time is to again imagine the earth as the source of life. Our goal should not be to consume but to be fully alive and awaken to our true calling as stewards and caretakers of this precious earth. Rewilding can help us do this.

The living earth is our natural habitat, and the more we are cut off from it, the deeper we sink into poor health, sadness, and ignorance. Perhaps the violence we see in our societies results from the ongoing violence to our home planet. As Luther Standing Bear so wisely said, "A lack of respect for green growing things soon leads to a lack of respect for people too."[7] How can we feel fully alive as a species if we are not only disconnected from our natural habitat but also actively destroying it?

In my early twenties, I took a job as a wilderness counselor to at-risk youth. I moved to the mountains of western North Carolina and lived outside with ten teenagers. Many had serious anger-management, self-regulation, and impulse-control issues. I lived and worked in that environment for three long years. It was grueling, dirty, frustrating, emotionally exhausting, and exhilarating. I led my groups on long canoe trips down remote rivers, sleeping on the banks, eating over fires, and drinking river water that tasted of sulfur even after mixing it with Kool-Aid and iodine tablets. The other counselors and I bonded, as we pulled together and relied on one another to get through the days. When the kids were asleep, we swapped stories about our crazy days until we fell asleep in our sleeping bags. In winter, we would wake to find our boots frozen so stiff that we couldn't get them back on our feet.

When I emerged from that journey and landed back home in stuffy Old Lyme, Connecticut, I felt bored, isolated, and deeply lonely, the way Monbiot had. I tried working as a substitute teacher and then as a waiter, but my soul said, *No*. I had to get out of the domesticated world of shopping malls and formal education, where people talked about investments, new cars, and local gossip. Life at camp had been brutal. I had faced bears, bullies, and rattlesnakes. I survived lightning storms in the middle of lakes, swimming with alligators, and eating fried Spam. Back home, I felt like nobody, just a dude in his late twenties trying to scratch together some money for rent and food. I didn't have a tribe, and I didn't feel very alive compared to the intensity I felt at camp.

My ecological boredom was closely tied to a sense of spiritual boredom. The years at camp had awakened a deep yearning to turn inward and find a place of peace and healing. One of the days when I was having a very difficult time at camp and felt at the end of my rope, I prayed to Spirit for help. At that exact moment, as tears streamed down my face, I looked up and a very large black bear stepped out of the rhododendrons ten feet in front of me. We locked eyes. Then that bear backed into the forest and was gone. I felt that my prayer had been answered.

In the local paper I found an advertisement for Kripalu Yoga classes and dropped by that evening for my first class. I found a space and got settled. As I closed my eyes and began to follow the teacher's instructions, something gave way in my heart. The pain of my time in the woods began to rise, tears started to flow, and I could feel a warm energy moving through me. It felt so good, and I felt so safe. The teacher led us through a series of postures, and my body opened. I was breathing. I was feeling. All the tightness and tension started to melt away.

When I opened my eyes after *Savasana*, Corpse Pose, the sun had set, and the full moon was shining brightly through the window, bathing the room in moonlight. My tears had dried on my face, and I felt refreshed. Kripalu Yoga felt like coming home.

Following the memory of that experience, I went on my own adventure, and I began to deepen my practice of yoga and meditation. The present-moment awareness, conscious breathing, and inner peace I found through these practices ultimately led me to Kripalu Center for Yoga & Health, where I began teaching yoga, met my wife, and settled down. In finding Kripalu, I not only found an inner space that was calling to me, I also found an ecological body that felt like home. The hills, valleys, lakes, streams, and fields of the Berkshires seemed to trigger almost a cellular feeling of being home and at ease. Arriving here, I experienced a love of place. Like biophilia, the love of nature and other beings, this "topophilia" let me know I was welcome and that I belonged.

The morning after my wife and I were married, I went outside to get something out of our used Subaru Outback. The car had come with a pin in the shape of a grizzly bear on the driver's visor, so we called the car "the Bear." That morning, as I approached the car, the interior lights were on and the driver's side door was open. I thought someone must have broken in during the night. Upon closer inspection, I noticed a muddy paw print with five claw marks on the door by the handle. It was a bear's paw print. One of my bear friends had gotten into the center console and eaten the granola bar that I had left there. The steering wheel, dashboard, and center console were covered with the dried film of bear saliva. A black bear had been sitting in the driver's seat of my car on the night of my wedding!

Over the years, the message of this bear visitation has become clearer to me. If I were interpreting a dream in which this happened, I would say that the bear was sitting in the driver's seat of my life and that bear energy is guiding me as I move along the road of life. When waking life becomes as magical as our dreaming life, when the wild visits us, even as we are seeking it, these are rare gifts indeed!

Perhaps you too have felt the presence of the sacred in nature. Feeling a sense of connection and a deepening relationship with the living earth, its landscapes, and other life-forms connects us with ways of being that are in our ancestral history. It doesn't take months or years of meditating outdoors to have an experience of connection with nature. Oftentimes it only takes a few minutes of sitting still and paying attention with curiosity.

Natural Mindfulness

As I write these words, I sit at my desk in the Berkshires, just a few miles from Kripalu, looking out my bedroom window onto my backyard. It's early spring. I take a deep breath and sigh, inviting my attention to rest in the present moment, taking in the beauty of the earth before me. The grass is still the color of hay, and the tree limbs are bare. The mountain that rises up into the sky before me is bathed in late afternoon sunlight, as is the shimmering little brook that flows at its base. The window is open and a light breeze is tickling the wind chimes in the crabapple tree outside. There is a stillness on the land and a quiet beauty. This is my spot, the place where I sit, ponder, write, and gaze (frequently) out the window, just as I did as a kid at school. I treasure these moments watching the robins look for worms and the mallards nesting in our marsh. From here I can watch the crabapple tree turn bright pink in May and the blueberry bushes blossom and fruit through the summer. This is where I watch river otters play and muskrats swim and where I listen to the turkeys gobble, the pileated woodpeckers call, and the woodcocks bleat.

Over the five years that we have lived at the foot of this little mountain, I have grown to care deeply for this land. I feel bonded to it. I have planted apple trees and blueberry bushes and watched over the years as our baby balsam has grown taller than us all. We put in gardens that feed us and year after year watch a family of robins struggle to bring their babies to maturity. I've seen bobcat, bear, fox, and coyote. Herds of deer bed down in the thicket, and families of grey and red squirrels, chipmunks, groundhogs, raccoons, and skunks prowl through our yard at night. On this land, my children run barefoot in the grass and look up at the great sky to see Canada geese honking, osprey soaring, and red-tailed hawks circling. Sometimes I look out this window and watch the children sitting quietly in the light from our only sun, as they enjoy a snack and wiggle their toes in the breeze. They abide in these moments much like other animals resting in the afternoon light, exuding a regal tranquility that mirrors the qualities of the living earth that holds them.

Mindfulness is the practice of bringing attention to what is happening in the present moment while letting go of judging the moment as good or bad. Mindfulness practice requires some detachment. To do it, we must rise above our thoughts, feelings, and sensations in order to engage in self-observation, or what we call "witness consciousness" in Kripalu Yoga. It's not that you stop feeling—quite the opposite—but rather that you make the choice to feel fully. You choose to breathe into whatever may be happening right now, instead of distracting yourself from it.

In mindful rewilding, mindfulness is a tool to train yourself to be here now, with the earth as it is, as you allow yourself to lean into pleasant experiences in nature and enjoy them fully. If you want to, you can follow anything that feels good, that pulls your attention into the experience of being fully alive. Over the years, I've found that the living earth offers these moments much more often than I once thought possible. As we develop the ability to be more present in our body and on the land, our senses begin to speak to us in ways that might surprise. Of course, there are plenty of uncomfortable sensations to be had along with the pleasant ones, such as intense heat and humidity, being wet and cold, insect bites that itch. We abide with these, too. In mindfulness practice, we observe that our experience is always changing, and we watch as our habitual patterns show themselves to see if we can respond rather than react to them. We notice the stories that run through our minds, like television shows, as we make up what might be happening. Our stories can be very compelling, even when we know they might not be true, and our stories may cause us to take action. Even in nature, outside our comfort zone, we may notice our minds spinning stories. Mindfulness practice can help strengthen the observer or witness or eagle vision, so that we can see our inner workings from a higher perspective, so that we can see through the manufactured stories and become more discerning in our actions.

When I get home from a long day at work, I take off my shoes and walk barefoot on the grass. I inspect the stream and look for animal tracks in the mud or the snow, depending on the season. I squat down and listen to the birds talking to one another, and I watch and listen to the great white pines whooshing in the evening breeze. In the winter, I walk barefoot through the snow and strip down to my boxer briefs and bathe in the ice-cold stream. But that's another story. After being in an office all day, dealing with computers, meetings, right angles, stale air, and constant social interactions, being in nature is the perfect balance. I don't have to be someone; I can just be. I don't have to focus my attention just here, as I do throughout the day when sending emails and holding meetings. Instead, I can let my senses open up and take in the miracle of trees, the flowing brook, the birds, clouds, wind, and the cool touch of the evening grass.

With my bodily senses totally immersed, my attention is absolutely in the present moment, though it is not focused. It is free to flow and to follow the beauty of the way nature moves. This is a natural form of mindfulness, in which I surrender to the presence of the living earth and allow her dance to carry me fully into the present moment.

In natural mindfulness, we come to the outdoors with no agenda, opening our senses and being entertained or entranced by the movement and qualities of the land, the land from which we sprang and the land that sustains us with every breath. We allow our attention to be called to things that bring us peace, joy, or awe. A flickering fire or a gentle breeze is a friendly companion and a doorway to meditation. There are so many ways to experience the wonder of now.

When I've been cooped up for too long, whether at the office or at home on the weekends, I tend to get anxious, irritable, and reactive. But whenever I step outside and take a deep breath, the fresh air immediately helps to shift my focus from my anxiety to the beauty of the land and all the things I am grateful for. When I feel cut off from the pulse of the earth and the seasons, cut off from fresh air and the uplifting presence of trees and other nonhuman life-forms, I notice myself become a bit callous and hard. The constant bombardment of problems and global catastrophes that my television, computer, and smartphone show me can sometimes overwhelm me. I wonder if much of the pain and suffering we see in the world today is the result of our being indoors too much, if they are the result of ecological and spiritual boredom. Exposure to the beauty and scale of nature, to its mountains, open spaces, and infinite sky always gives me a healthy perspective.

I am not going to be in this body forever. The universe is so big, and life so precious and fragile. Our species can reclaim our once wild selves and appreciate once again our natural habitats, which are the best catalysts there ever were for mindfulness and perspective.

Earth Time

When I was a therapeutic wilderness counselor at a camp in North Carolina, the staff and students would all travel down to Florida for three-week canoe expeditions. These were usually pretty rigorous journeys, both physically and spiritually. The kids didn't always get along or follow the rules, yet the success of the trip depended on everyone's ability to work as a team. When that broke down, things could get miserable fast.

Still and all, just being on the river in canoes, we'd slip into another kind of time. After about a week on the river, we'd get into a flow. I used to call it "river time." The character of the liquid road we were traveling seemed to alter our perception of time. In some ways and for certain periods, there was no time. I'd be reading the currents, watching the skies, listening to what was up ahead, living very much in the moment, which I think is something inherent in rewilding. In his book *Affluence Without Abundance*, anthropologist James Suzman compares the lived experience of time in hunter-gatherer societies with that of people living in modern societies:

> This is one of the big, big differences between us and
> hunter-gatherer cultures. And I'm amazed that actually
> more anthropologists haven't written about it. Everything in
> our lives is kind of future-oriented. For example, we might
> get a college degree so we can get a job, so that we can get
> a pension. For farmers it was the same way. They planted
> seeds for the harvest and to store. But for hunter-gatherers,
> everything was present-oriented. All their effort was focused
> on meeting an immediate need. They were absolutely
> confident that they would be able to get food from their
> environment when they needed it. So, they didn't waste
> time storing or growing food. This lifestyle created a very
> different perspective on time.[8]

In yoga, Buddhism, and other contemplative traditions, mindful awareness is cultivated through the regular practice of meditation. But I have noticed, and perhaps you have as well, that when I spend extended periods of time in nature's elements, a state of flowing aware-ness in the present moment emerges organically. Suzman says, "Today people [in Western societies] go to mindfulness classes, yoga classes, and dancing clubs, just so for a moment they can live in the present. The Bushmen live that way all the time!"[9]

The widespread interest today in yoga, meditation, and connect-ing with nature reflects our need to escape the ceaseless challenge of contending with the demons of future and past that is life in modern society. The ancient Greeks spoke of two kinds of time. One they called Chronos, which is linear time, cutting straight into the future like an arrow and leaving behind the past. The other they called Kairos, which is circular time, ever spiraling round and round. In Kairos time, we find the circle rather than the line. In nature, things move in circles. Each seasonal cycle brings back familiar beings, sights, sounds, smells, textures, and flavors. We age as we are carried through these circles. Many indigenous cultures studied the way life moves in great spirals, and they had faith in the curative properties of spiral energy.

In rewilding, we enter the spiraling waters of Kairos, an opportunity to rest our weary minds from their burdensome preoccupation with the future and the past. We return home to the eternal now as we experience it through our earthly bodies in relationship with our dynamic and beautiful home planet.

Mindfully communing with the forest is a profound practice of self-discovery. Every tree, stone, plant, insect, movement of wind, shaft of light, patch of shadow, and flying bird have something to teach us if we can empty our minds and open ourselves to them. During a summer solstice retreat, I asked each member of the group to seek out a spot in nature and to sit there for thirty minutes and simply to observe their surroundings. Afterward, when the group came back together to tell their stories, one young woman shared the following.

She found herself staring at a standing dead tree, rotten inside and barely holding itself up. As she stayed with her curiosity about this tree, she began to think of her father. She shared that her dad, like the tree, had managed to stay upright and breathing long after he had stopped growing or actively engaging with life. He hung on to his life after he had stopped really living. Being with the tree, she was able to see the ways in which it was a host for other kinds of life. She saw that it had its own wisdom and teachings to share, and she found comfort in the tree and some healing of the expectations she had of her father.

Mindfulness is a discipline. Because the mind's nature is mercurial, it wants to move, imagine, analyze, strategize, judge, interpret, and often to worry. To practice mindfulness is to yoke the mind and train its attention to the experience happening right now. It is a practice of directly perceiving reality (as much as is possible with our limited senses), of rising above and letting go of the mental filters that color our experiences. It is a practice of being with life just as it is. In some forms of mindfulness, we close our eyes and direct our awareness internally, to the vast territories of consciousness, sensation, and space in the mind-body. In the yoga tradition, this is called *pratyahara*, or inward sensing. Other forms of mindfulness open awareness to interface directly with the external realm of the senses, with the vast territories of earth's elements (earth, fire, water, air, and space) moving, expressing, and flowing through nature.

The practice of mindfulness can help to illuminate both your inner and outer perception of reality. Your outer perception, your senses, which perceive the world, developed in relationship with the environments our ancestors evolved in. Your sense of hearing developed over millions of years in relationship with the songs of birds, the trickle of water, the crackling of fire, and the many other manifestations of the life force on earth. The smallest sound can convey an abundance of information that can be life-saving—the sudden silence of birdsong, the quiet trill of a squirrel, the snap of a twig by a predator.

The same is true of all our other senses. They developed in nature, too. Being mindful of your perceptions of the living earth helps move you out of the mental plane, where we easily abstract and objectify nature, and into an embodied experience of being woven into the fabric of life on this planet. When this happens, you have the opportunity to come home to your body and life presence in a powerful way. You have the chance to be soothed by a very old and wise friend, a being who has always fed, clothed, and sheltered you. When you begin to feel a part of your landscape and relate to the other life-forms around you as your relatives, rather than as inanimate or less-evolved objects, you begin to feel more connection. No longer estranged from your home planet, your great earthly mother, you begin to feel part of something much greater than yourself.

Through the path of mindful rewilding, we bring awareness to our breath, which helps us get out of our discursive "monkey minds," the incessant chattering of thoughts, and brings our awareness instead to our body and the present moment. As we connect with the body, we connect to our senses, and when we connect with our senses, we begin to wake up. It's as if we are dreaming our lives away when we allow our attention to be absorbed in our internal mental chatter. Our hunting and gathering ancestors attended to their senses and interacted with a dynamic living earth. Our fascination with our smartphones and screens is an externalization of our monkey mind's predisposition to be anywhere other than here now. When we awaken to our senses and their engagement with the living earth, we see trees as other living things with whom we share this planet, and we recognize other human beings as our kindred. We see this precious earth as our extended self, and we receive the holy air as a gift, as the gift of life. These experiences can change us, forever. When we take these practices into nature and see and feel the presence of this living earth in all its many wondrous forms, it is possible to glimpse Eden and Shambhala, the true paradise that earth can be.

NATURAL MINDFULNESS

The practice of mindfulness has significant effects on the structure of the brain. Scientific studies show that mindfulness practice reduces the size of the amygdala, the watchdog region of the brain that is involved in processing fear, emotion, and our response to stress.[10] Mindfulness has also been shown to increase the size of the prefrontal cortex, the region of the brain associated with executive decision-making, planning, and strategy. In addition, mindfulness practice appears to decrease the connectivity of the amygdala to the rest of the brain, while increasing the connectivity of the prefrontal cortex, which appears to reduce reactivity to stressful situations and enhance thoughtful response.

But how does it work? When we sit and bring our attention to our breathing, the mind tends to wander. We watch our breath for a few moments, and then we start thinking about dinner or something that happened at work. When we notice our attention has drifted, we come back to the breath. We may find that when we notice our mind has drifted, there is a reaction, such as, *Come on! I am bad at meditating! Why can't I stay with my breath?* This is where mindfulness becomes truly profound. At that moment, we also witness our response to noticing that our attention has wandered: *Oh, I just judged my wandering mind. What good does that do? Let me just let that judgment go and return to my breath.* Rather than reacting to the fact that the mind wandered, we observe the reaction with compassion and then come back to the practice, to our breath. With enough practice, mindfulness becomes a habit and begins to show up when we are not on our meditation cushion, or log or boulder if we are mindfully rewilding outside. This natural mindfulness begins to show up in our relationships, work, and life in general.

Imagine that you are walking mindfully through the forest and you suddenly see a snake in the middle of the trail. Now, let's say that you are afraid of snakes and have a whole identity built around this fear. But let's say that you've also been practicing breath-based mindful meditation a lot since the last time you saw a snake. This time when you see the snake, you have an instant startle response and you back up, but then you immediately drop into the place of observing your own reaction. You notice the fight-or-flight response, and you pause. The snake is ten feet away and shows no interest in you. Instead of running away, you keep a safe distance and observe the snake. Rather than being controlled by habitual responses, you assess the situation. You are not in danger. For the first time in your life, you are not being controlled by your fear, and you begin to experience a sense of curiosity instead of terror. The reality of the snake and your stories about snakes are different. You take a deep breath and watch the snake. As you spend time in its presence, you begin to create a new neural pathway in your brain, as you begin to associate this encounter with interest and curiosity instead of terror and reactivity.

How many other ingrained fears might you reshape in this life with mindfulness? Can you see how you might apply this natural mindfulness to situations at work or with your family? This practice can be transformational. For rewilding, the practice of mindfulness is essential. It allows your reintegration as a human being into earth's wild places in a way that brings greater calm, clarity, connection, and confidence.

You don't need to be a hard-core outdoor person, a wilderness guide, an ancestral skills expert, a proficient meditator or yogi to take a step in the direction of your wild, alive, and wise self. You need only to start with this breath and a desire to connect with life. In the chapters ahead, we will explore some of the simple, time-tested practices and insights that have come down to us through the wisdom traditions of yoga, Buddhism, and indigenous cultures. Remembering how to breathe with awareness, listen to the earth, walk with awareness, and kindle a sacred fire can open doorways into another state of consciousness and way of being. Sometimes what we need is not more but less. Sometimes we need to let go and let nature show us the way.

The most important of all the creatures are the winged, for they are nearest to the heavens and are not bound to the earth, as are the four-legged or little crawling people. . . . They see everything that happens on the earth.

BLACK ELK

2

EYES OF THE EAGLE

The Journey Inward Leads Us Outward

Rewilding practices increase your awareness of the outdoors and the world around you, and they also increase your sense of being at home within your own body. The awareness and connection mindful rewilding has given me has shifted how I see everything.

Sometimes when I break from the desk work at my job, I like to take walks on the beautiful grounds of the retreat center. A family of red-tailed hawks nest on the property every year. During my walks, my mind is often absorbed by work dramas and problems, but the shrill call of the hawks circling high above pierces through that mental activity and brings me quickly back into the present moment. The hawks' message is to wake up, to come into the moment, to look sharp and see inner and outer life from a higher level. Looking up at the hawks soaring, I adopt their higher perspective, and it helps me gain insight into whatever's going on for me at the earth level. Sometimes this inner outlook has also given me glimpses of lofty new perspectives on our interconnectedness and the greater universe. Of course, I'm not alone in this point of view.

In 1971, *Apollo 14* astronaut Edgar Mitchell became the sixth man to walk on the moon. During his trip back to Earth, he gazed out the window of the spacecraft and saw our planet, its moon, and its sun turning in the vast cosmic sky, as the space module slowly spun round and round. As he gazed out, he had a profound spiritual experience, a life-changing experience:

> I realized that matter in our universe was created in star systems, and that the molecules in my body and the molecules in the spacecraft and the molecules in my partner's body, were prototypes, or manufactured, in some ancient generation of star, and the recognition then that we're all a part of the same stuff. We're all one.[1]

Along with this sense of oneness, Mitchell felt a powerful ecstasy in his mind and body.

After he returned to Earth, Edgar described his experience to religious scholars and anthropologists, wondering if they knew of other such experiences from religious or mystical texts. They described a similar state, called *savikalpa samadhi* in Patanjali's Yoga Sutras, one of the seminal texts in the yoga tradition.

Savikalpa samadhi is a state of deep meditation that is supported by concentration on an object, which in Mitchell's case was the blue-green orb of our living planet, floating against the backdrop of the infinite universe. Other astronauts, including many who have spent time on the International Space Station (ISS), have had similarly powerful experiences of oneness followed by a corresponding sense of responsibility for our fragile planet. One of the favorite pastimes of orbiting astronauts is what they call "Earth gazing." From their home in the ISS, they look at Earth's thin blue line of atmosphere against the horizon, observing thunderstorms and the aurora borealis dance across the planet's surface. These experiences have led to a "cognitive shift in awareness" that is linked to "the experience of seeing firsthand the reality that the Earth is in space," which author Frank White calls "the overview effect." He writes:

> My hypothesis was that being in space, you would see and know something experientially that we have been

trying to understand intellectually for thousands of years. That is, that the Earth is a whole system, everything on it is connected, and we're a part of it.[2]

Isn't it unexpected and fascinating that the biggest discovery from the Apollo missions was less about the moon and more about how we think about Earth? It was the process of looking back at our home from that lofty perspective for the first time, of seeing it as a single, self-contained miracle, that allowed our species to realize that the one-ness mystical and spiritual traditions have spoken about for thousands of years is objectively and scientifically true. The "blue marble" image taken during *Apollo 17*, the final manned mission to the moon, forever changed the way we see our planet. It inspired astronomer and astrophysicist Carl Sagan to write:

> Look again at that dot. That's here. That's home. That's us. On it everyone you love, everyone you know, everyone you ever heard of, every human being who ever was, lived out their lives. The aggregate of our joy and suffering, thousands of confident religions, ideologies, and economic doctrines, every hunter and forager, every hero and coward, every creator and destroyer of civilization, every king and peasant, every young couple in love, every mother and father, hopeful child, inventor and explorer, every teacher of morals, every corrupt politician, every "superstar," every "supreme leader," every saint and sinner in the history of our species lived there—on a mote of dust suspended in a sunbeam. [3]

After his profound experience in outer space, Edgar Mitchell spent the rest of his life exploring inner space, the realm of consciousness itself. He founded the Institute of Noetic Sciences, an organization "dedicated to supporting individual and collective transformation through consciousness research, transformative learning, and engaging a global community in the realization of our human potential." This brilliant US Navy test pilot, with a degree from MIT, who had studied astrophysics at Harvard and helped problem-solve the rescue of *Apollo 13*, was among the world's most elite group of human explorers. He was in many ways the epitome of an objective scientist. Yet Edgar Mitchell and other space explorers tell us of the profound experiences they've had viewing Earth from orbit.

This remarkable phenomenon of the overview effect caught the attention of other scientists and has spawned new research on the mind and behavior. At the University of Pennsylvania's Positive Psychology Center, scientists are studying the overview effect to better understand the emotions that astronauts from many countries and different cultures share.[4] Perhaps the study of this powerful positive shift in awareness will contribute to humanity, in all our diversity, awakening to our interdependence. Perhaps this understanding can inform our actions, including global cooperative efforts to address issues such as climate change and habitat and species loss.

Of course, we don't need to physically travel to outer space to experience our interconnectedness. We need only to approach our living earth mindfully wherever we are. When we soar high enough in our awareness, we can see above the trees; we can see the world as it truly is, the truth that all life on earth is one, inextricably bound together. This is precisely what yogis and meditators, shamans and wisdom keepers, have experienced through the practices of mindful breathing and being present. These practices allow us to rise above the swirling drama of our mental activity and emotions, to see and enter the abiding awareness that remains still and calm. This awareness guides us to act skillfully through it all. Spiritual practitioners have made the journey inward that astronauts have made while soaring beyond the earth. Both have freed our limited human perspective to expand and to take in the totality of life on earth.

> Where we had thought to travel outward, we will
> come to the center of our own existence. And where
> we had thought to be alone, we will be with all the
> world. **JOSEPH CAMPBELL**[5]

Edgar Mitchell's journey speaks to the way in which our innate desire to explore the world outside, to see what is over the next hill, around the corner, and over the horizon, inevitably takes us inside, to the center of our own existence. It seems we can't explore the outer world without also expanding the dimensions of our inner world.

Mitchell's story also illustrates what I sometimes call "the slingshot effect": when we journey outward, in the realm of matter, our senses eventually reverse direction and propel our attention inward, to the source of consciousness itself. Inward reflection builds a strong sensitivity and a heightened awareness that can propel us into a deep, renewed relationship with the world of the senses and the living earth. After a yoga or meditation practice, for instance, you will likely find your senses heightened when you walk outside. Because your perception is clearer, you can appreciate the wonder of nature more easily.

Mindfulness Rewilded

> As great as the infinite space beyond is the space
> within the lotus of the heart. Both heaven and earth
> are contained in that inner space, both fire and air,
> sun and moon, lightning and stars. Whether we know
> it in this world or know it not, everything is contained
> in that inner space.   **THE CHANDOGYA UPANISHAD**

As someone inside "the mindfulness industry," I have observed that yoga has become as deprived of nature as the rest of society. With our rubber-soled shoes, yoga mats, and indoor practice spaces, modern humans move from one nature-disconnected space to another. Even during those rare moments between the car and the studio, we wear shoes that prevent contact with the ground beneath our feet. Yet the practices of yoga and meditation were born in the mountains, forests, and deserts of Asia.

A few years ago, I attended a yoga conference in Manhattan, a few floors up at the midtown Hilton. After my second yoga class in a stuffy, windowless room, with hundreds of yogis in spandex moving about on rubber mats, I experienced a moment of cognitive dissonance. I love yoga—it is a powerful beautiful practice—and I believe that the widespread increase in yoga and mindfulness practice is profoundly positive. However, something about this scenario didn't seem quite right to me—or quite right *for* me.

Not long after, at a yoga and recovery conference at Kripalu, my friend Tim Walsh, an avid outdoorsman and recovery coach, expressed my own thoughts when he said, "Folks, we're standing on rubber mats inside a temperature-controlled room on the second floor of a giant brick building. How much more disconnected from the earth can you get!" His words rang inside me, and at that moment, something in my core woke up. I had felt this disconnect for years, and now it was time to do something about it.

I had dreamed for many years of somehow bridging the worlds of meditation, yoga, and mindfulness with rewilding. When I finally started to research the connections between nature and mindfulness practices, I ended up creating programs for students at Kripalu that immersed us in forests and fields while practicing. I wanted to help people become conscious of their inner nature while out in nature and to help them see the importance of conserving our natural environments—the primal parts of ourselves. How did yoga and meditation, wild practices designed to awaken, empower, and enlighten, become so disconnected from the enlivening power and the beauty of the living earth? Because yoga and mindfulness have profound benefits for well-being, they have also been co-opted and commercialized. Products have proliferated—the mats and clothing, the snacks and the food, the shoes and the hats. Our economy is driven by the consumption of things that must be extracted from the earth and produced and marketed and sold. As yoga and mindfulness became imbedded in modern culture's mostly indoor lifestyle, these ancient practices also became cut off from the presence of the wind, sun, moon, and life of the living earth.

When we disconnect from the living earth, we lose the life-affirming wisdom that is found outdoors. If we consider the fact that we are an evolutionary expression of the evolving earth, then our own self-awareness can be thought of as the self-awareness of the living earth itself.

Which is a pretty powerful idea to ponder! And it means that human rewilding can lead to a rewilding of our spirit, a *reinspiriting* of our essential nature.

Pacification or Liberation?

Yoga and mindfulness today are often used to help people invite calm and to support greater self-regulation and impulse control in stressful situations. But just as I'm concerned about their commodification, I'm also concerned that these ancient practices are being used as pacifiers to help people put up with the negative effects of modern society, because these ancient practices are also the tools for true liberation from the root causes of our distress.

To be clear, yoga, meditation, and mindfulness are extremely valuable practices. The abilities to take a deep breath and step back from the fight-or-flight response, to self-soothe, and to know when to practice self-care, these are all critical tools for living consciously.

I am reminded of an episode of the old television show *Kung Fu*, in which a martial arts master, played by David Carradine, is taken prisoner and forced into manual labor under the blazing sun. Labeled a troublemaker, he is put into a hot box, a cast-iron oven with an unbearably fierce temperature. In the box is another man who is panicked by their dangerous situation. Carradine calmly teaches the man how to meditate, to slow his breathing and witness his thoughts. At the end of the day they are released, and both emerge from the box alert and calm, much to the surprise of their captors.

A more recent real-life example is the group of boys on a soccer team in Thailand who were stranded for almost two weeks in a complex network of flooded tunnels. They learned to meditate from their coach, who had lived in a Buddhist monastery for ten years. They sat in the darkness, not knowing if anyone would come to their aid, and they stayed calm and connected to one another. They were all ultimately saved by a team of divers who risked their own lives in the effort.

Meditation is a powerful antidote to fear and the modern daily stresses that can harm our health if left unchecked. Meditation can even save your life. But if you are under duress, the first thing to check is whether you can get out of it. See if the door to the hot box can be opened. Look for the escape route in the cave. If a change in the circumstances is possible, the wise action is to eliminate the cause of suffering first, and meditate later.

As a species, we often don't even know that we are in a hot box or a dangerous cave. The stress of modern life is ubiquitous, so a change of environment may not even seem like an option. And, of course, not everyone can get away from their circumstances or difficulties. Not everyone has easy access to pristine natural places. Many can't afford to travel to a place with fresh air and water.

I hope that the steps I teach here for connecting with the living earth will open doors for everyone. The sunlight, the movement of air, the presence of the earth that is solid and stable even in asphalt, the dandelion coming up through a crack in the pavement, all can be entries into a wilder, more conscious, more awakened life.

Learning to Soar

> The highest spiritual practice is self-observation
> without judgment.   SWAMI KRIPALU

One of the cornerstones of yoga is the practice of cultivating witness consciousness, which in the Kripalu Yoga tradition is a practice of self-observation without judgment. The witness is our ability to watch our own bodily sensations, urges, thoughts, feelings, and mental stories without judgment or reactivity. It's not that you stop feeling; quite the opposite, it's that you make the choice to feel fully. You choose to breathe into whatever may be happening right now rather than distracting yourself from it. In many indigenous cultures, this level of consciousness is associated with birds who soar, such as the condor, eagle, and hawk. Cultivating this objective state of awareness is at the heart of mindfulness practice, and it is also a powerful tool in our work to become intimate with the living earth.

Meditation is the practice of focusing attention on the contents of the present moment while cultivating a nonjudgmental attitude.

Some of the earliest meditators were ancient hunters sitting for long periods of time while hunting to feed their tribe. Hunting involves not only tracking an animal and knowing its routines but also sitting absolutely still for hours while paying close attention to all movement on the land around you. Of course, in hunter-gatherer cultures, hunting is essential for survival, but for many people in modern societies, hunting is not practical or desirable.

You can still enjoy the benefits of sitting outdoors regularly and inviting your attention to rest on the more-than-human world around you, on its movement and on the qualities of the land. All you need to do is to find a location outdoors that is easy to get to every day where you can allow yourself some time to simply sit and observe what is happening. The centering practice I will share can help you. If you commit to this daily practice, you will become a witness to how your land changes through the seasons and the years. You will begin to know more about the plants and animals that share the land, and you will even get to know individuals as time goes by.

At Kripalu, we have a red squirrel who lives in the hedge that runs all along the south-facing side of the building. Red squirrels are high-energy critters, full of spunk and attitude. One of this squirrel's ears has a big chunk missing out of it, perhaps from a dispute with another red squirrel. I've watched this little guy for the past year and call him "One Ear." I get such a burst of happiness when I see him. He's always on the move. It is very sweet and rewarding to get to know an individual wild animal.

Recognition and awareness of individual wild animals can open our hearts, as we feel the animals' struggles and losses and mourn their passing. One year, a red fox made a den on the property at Kripalu. All through the summer that fox made herself known, hunting rabbits that lived in the hedge to feed her pups (much to the horror of some guests) and moving freely through the grounds at all hours of the day. We all loved to watch for her and share stories of her exploits. At the end of the season, we were saddened to find her body by the road; she had been struck by a car. She was not simply roadkill to us, a random member of a common species; she was an individual with a life story.

We had had the opportunity to share a part of our lives with her and to know about her.

Nature connection and nature meditation open our hearts to all lives on the land. With the expansion of awareness comes a deepening of feelings and attachment, not a dependent attachment but a loving appreciation. We need this experience to awaken an ethic of steward-ship and responsibility for our world.

To prepare for nature meditation, it's essential to learn how to invite your attention out of the past and future and in to the dynamic, breathing, ever-changing qualities of the living earth in this present moment. Let's explore a practice with which you can center yourself outdoors. I invite you to adopt this practice and to use it every day, in your favorite spot outdoors whenever possible. It is a first step in your mindful rewilding. Even if you can't practice outside every day, I invite you to use it wherever you are, wherever you can. If you are at home, you can sit in front of a plant, some herbs, or a burning candle, something to connect you with the living earth.

CENTERING

At the beginning of any outdoor experience, I pause to center myself. Centering just means inviting your attention to rest in the present moment. I like to close my eyes and focus internally. This brief rest of the senses actually sharpens them so that when I refocus my awareness outward, I perceive the earth around me. Becoming centered shows respect and gratitude for the earth and intensifies our time in nature.

Take a soft, deep breath in, and let your exhalation be twice as long as your inhalation. This stimulates the relaxation response in the body. Continue to breathe softly in through the nose and exhale long and slow. Each time you exhale, feel your mind emptying and your body relaxing. See if you can enjoy the sensations in your body as you deeply breathe in and out. The present moment is the only moment. Stay in it.

When you are ready, release control of the breath and notice how you feel. When you feel complete, open your eyes. Look around and take a few moments to observe your surroundings.

A natural outcome of practicing this over time is an experience of connection with yourself, the people around you, and your environment. When you pay attention to your present-moment experience as it unfolds in your environment, it is easy to see that you are a part of your world. It's when we get stuck in our heads, walking through life on autopilot, allowing the unconscious mind to move us through our days, that it's easy to miss the many ways we affect and are affected by our environment and the life-forms we share our world with.

NATURE MEDITATION

Find a place outside near where you live, a place you can get to easily and regularly for your nature meditation. Perhaps there is a tree or a stone you can rest against and get to know. Pay attention to your intuition, and trust that you will be drawn to a spot that has good energy, a place that feels right. Allow yourself at least fifteen minutes in this place; thirty to forty-five minutes is even better.

Once you're in your spot, find a comfortable seat, and when you are ready, close your eyes and draw a soft breath in through the nose. Hold the breath in for a moment or two and then exhale slowly and mindfully through the nose, so that the exhalation is twice as long as the inhalation. Repeat this breathwork three to five times, until you begin to feel your whole being relaxing into the present moment.

Feel your sitz bones, the two boney knobs at the base of your pelvis, rooted in the earth. Begin to feel the crown of your head lifting up toward the sky, drawing your spine long. Soften your jaw and forehead, and relax your abdomen. Begin to notice your breath and the gentle pulse as it moves in and out through the nose. Invite your attention to stay with your breath, allowing your awareness to float on the gentle waves moving into and out of your body. Be a compassionate observer, taking in whatever might be moving within your awareness. Whenever you notice your mind drift away, return to the sensation of your breath. Notice the bodily sensations, thoughts, and emotions as you sit and breathe. Let them all come and go.

When you are ready, open your eyes. Shift your attention from your breath to any movement you see in your environment. Let your attention rest in the flow of movement you are immersed in—the subtle vibration of the grass, leaves bobbing on the breeze, flickering light on flowing water, the swirl of snowflakes. Take as much time as you'd like to experience what is happening in the moment.

Nature meditation is an invitation to enjoy the beauty of nature in each moment. Even sitting inside, you can center yourself and then gaze out a window. The more relaxed and still you can be, the more likely you are to notice activity around you. The animals who frequent the land around your sitting spot will eventually start moving about, and in time, you will be gifted with their presence and gain a window into their world. If you practice nature meditation consistently, over time you will learn much about the land you live on.

When beginning to establish a meditation practice, you may feel that there is a right way and a wrong way to meditate or that you should be able to stop your thoughts and experience perfect peace, emptiness, and equanimity. These are unrealistic expectations to put on yourself. Over time and with practice, the mind will be able to enter greater and greater degrees of absorption—but to begin, you need simply to attend to the breath and to be kind and gentle with yourself.

When we practice cultivating the perspective of the witness, we notice sensations, thought patterns, and habitual reactions. We begin to lift our awareness up above our patterns and habits and take on a process of self-study, which in yoga is called *svadhyaya*. From up above, we can see the weather inside, the emotional storms and mental stories that play over and over again in the mind, as well as the patterns of action we take, which may or may not be useful. The practice of witness consciousness gives us a higher perspective on life, the same way that being suspended outside our planet's atmosphere allowed astronauts to see the interconnectedness of our world. As we learn to be compassionate observers and connect more intimately with the earth, it makes sense that we might also grow wiser in our relationships with our home planet.

WITNESS IN THE WOODS

Cultivating witness consciousness is essential to the practice of mindfulness. Try this brief exercise to become more mindful of the present moment. The next time you are getting ready to head out on a walk or into a park or the woods, take a moment to pause and draw a deep breath in and out with a gentle sigh. Close your eyes and begin to breathe a slow but steady breath, in and out. Imagine that your awareness is a boat floating on these slow, steady waves of breath. Notice how fast your mind is going, and see the speedometer in your mind slowing down, gradually and smoothly, until it rests at 0 miles per hour. You are here.

Now, open your eyes and slowly and mindfully take in the colors, contours, and movements of the earth. Notice what you can hear, such as the sounds of wind, leaves, birds. How does the air smell? Can you feel the temperature on your skin? Notice the land all around you, and reach out with your awareness to feel the pulse of life you are embedded in. Be still for a few more moments before you start to walk into the land ahead of you. Open your senses to feel the life around you and within you.

Before your first step, set an intention to remain present and connected to your breath. Then take your first step. Go slowly, and as you take each step, walk with awareness. With each mindful step, feel the earth beneath your feet. Let your heel, sole, and toes connect with the ground, with its ancient strength and solidity. You might consider each step a caress of the earth and extend gratitude as you move over land. If your mind drifts away from the breath and your steps, just bring your attention back to the land and your breath. Be a mindful witness of the living earth.

As you practice this way of being on the land, you will notice things you didn't before. You will also become more aware of yourself so that every time you enter the land, your feeling of belonging will grow. Pause often and take in anything that fascinates you. Enjoy the wonder of each moment.

The Breath

In my own journey into mindfulness and rewilding, I have been deeply influenced by the writings of Buddhist master Thich Nhat Hanh. Thay, as he is called by his students, encourages a simple path to mindfulness which emphasizes conscious breathing, among other things. When I began to connect deeply with my own breath, I felt I had found the master key, the secret I had been waiting for, the practice that would open all doors. Thay taught me that the breath is always rising and falling in the present moment, so, when you bring your attention to it, you have an anchor in the now. No matter how many millions of times your attention wanders away from the present moment, the breath is always there to bring you back.

As I began to establish a more consistent relationship with my own breath, I had an immediate and powerful experience of being connected with the life force on earth, the pulsing, ever-moving atmosphere that all breathing beings share. The more I practiced mindful breathing, the more attuned I felt to the earth around me, the air, the animals, and the elements. Breathing with awareness, I realized that I enjoyed the way it felt to breathe deeply. The breath slowed me down and helped me get out of my head and into my feeling body. I started taking long walks in the woods while focusing on staying with my breath. I started to feel more awe. I noticed more of the details in the forest. Where I once saw the forest as a blur of generalized categories—trees, stones, ground, sky—now I noticed individual pine trees, carpet mosses, cup fungi, drops of water. And beyond that, I was also sensing the interconnection of these life-forms in the forest.

There was no specific point of focus for this sense of connection; rather, it was an embodied experience, a felt sense that the air I was breathing, along with the wind, the trees, and the earth, were not distinct and separate objects but interdependent and living subjects. I was sensing the intersecting ripples of energy in which I was immersed. Staying with my breathing and being mindful of my embodied experience was helping me to expand my awareness and receive the grandeur and majesty of the earth. I felt more human than I had ever felt before.

Breathing with awareness can open many doors. Some take us inward, and others guide our attention outward—but inward and outward are both parts of a single spectrum of awareness. Nature dwells in both directions, not just outside us. Our inner world is also nature. Our minds and bodies are manifestations of the evolution of the living earth.

One of the miraculous things about breathing is that it truly is a constant reminder that we exist in a constant state of interbeing with the rest of life. When we breathe, we bring the atmosphere of the planet into our bodies, and when we exhale, we send our unique essence back into the ever-swirling breath of life on earth. The air we are breathing right now was on the other side of the planet just four or five days ago.[6] This means that the air we exhale right now could become part of a cat in France or a tree in Iceland in just a few days. This knowledge and this sense that the act of breathing puts us in relationship with all other living things on earth is ancient. The Lakota refer to the enveloping atmosphere as "the holy air," or *woniya* in their language, and they believe that it carries the messages of *Wakan Tanka*, or the Great Spirit across the world.[7] The smoke that rises from the sacred pipes reveals the movement of the Great Spirit, whose medium is the holy winds.

In his book *The Spell of the Sensuous*, David Abram explains that the invisible currents of air in which our bodies are immersed have been considered by many cultures to be the essence of life-giving spirit. In the yoga tradition, the breath is known as *prana*, which means "life energy." The art of breathing with skill involves balancing the energies of life present in the body, and even accumulating a charge of prana in the mind-body to enhance a greater sustained aliveness. A simple question you can ask yourself after the mindful walking or breathing of rewilding is, Do I feel more alive?

To breathe is to be alive and connected. When you recognize how vital the air is to life and how powerful the practice of mindful breathing is for well-being, it is easy to feel gratitude and awe for the mystery of the breath. Unfortunately, many people do not bring awareness to their breathing or ponder the necessity of clean air or the gift of each breath and the life it makes possible. Air and water are vital elements.

They exist within us and we within them. In the closed system that is planet Earth, how can we be well if our air and water are polluted? How can the earth be well?

In Patanjali's Yoga Sutras, the very first word is *atha*, which means "now" in Sanskrit. In classical Indian literature, the first word in a sacred text is often the most important, and so in the case of the Yoga Sutras, that would mean the most important concept in the whole book is encapsulated in the word *now*. In yoga, when the mind, the breath, and the posture or movement of the body are integrated and aligned, the practitioner experiences this unity. The only way to achieve this state of integrated functioning is to hold our awareness squarely in the present moment, concentrating on what we are doing and using the breath and the sensations in the body as anchors. Think about how many times in a day you go on autopilot, how many times you allow your unconscious mind to take control of what you are doing. Maybe you're eating lunch and looking at your phone. You're eating, but you aren't fully conscious of what you're eating. Or perhaps you are hiking in the woods, but your mind is elsewhere, thinking about work or some other dilemma or worry. You are missing all the life around you.

Just being outside in nature can have a beneficial effect on your stress level, help elevate your mood, and even help you become more alert and alive. These positive benefits are enhanced exponentially when we are mindful in nature. And though our minds will always wander when we are physically wandering, we can take hold of our breath and return, time and again, to the miracle of the moment. If we are truly paying attention, there is always something to notice and learn from, whether a tiny bird, a flowering bud, or an autumn leaf covered in frost. The gifts are all around us; we need only open our eyes to see them.

Sit Under a Tree and Breathe

Thich Nhat Hanh's style of mindful breathing requires only attention and a willingness to gently deepen and feel your breath. It is more accessible than the elaborate yogic pranayama practices I have learned.

Thay was influenced by the Buddha's approach, which he offered to his disciples long ago:

> A monk having gone to the forest, to the foot of a tree
> or to an empty place, sits down, with his legs crossed,
> keeps his body erect and his mindfulness alert. Ever
> mindful he breathes in, and mindful he breathes out.
> Breathing in a long breath, he knows, "I am breathing
> in a long breath"; breathing out a long breath, he knows,
> "I am breathing out a long breath"; breathing in a short
> breath, he knows "I am breathing in a short breath";
> breathing out he knows, "I am breathing out a short
> breath."   SATIPATTHANA SUTTA[8]

The Buddha taught that the breath is a powerful tool for cultivating mindfulness, and that he suggested practicing mindful breathing while sitting under a tree. The Buddha himself attained enlightenment sitting under the bodhi tree. *Bodhi* means "awake," and under the bodhi tree, a man named Siddhartha became "the awakened one," or the Buddha. We don't know the role of the tree in the Buddha's sitting or the role of the forest network the tree was a part of, but we do know that as Homo sapiens our relationship with trees goes back at least a few hundred thousand years. We evolved living in relationship with trees; we have been shaped by their presence. Perhaps the presence of the bodhi tree, its shade, the sound of its leaves and branches moving in the breeze, its presence as a living being, helped the Buddha to drop into a profound state of self-realization. Studies have certainly shown that views of nature and even the presence of plants in our homes and offices, can reduce stress, improve immune function, and restore our fatigued attention spans.[9] When you consider how long we as a species have been sharing an intimate relationship with trees, it is no wonder we feel comforted and supported in mindfulness in their presence.

Contentment

Thay simplifies the Buddha's teaching on mindful breathing even further:

> (Inhale) Breathing in, I know I am breathing in.
> (Exhale) Breathing out, I know I am breathing out.
> (Inhale) Dwelling deeply in the present moment.
> (Exhale) I know this is a wonderful moment.[10]

You may like to try this simple exercise the next time you feel stressed or overwhelmed. I have always found it to be a sweet and powerful practice for supporting mindfulness and bringing the witness consciousness or objectivity back into focus. When you practice it, you may notice that it conveys contentment, which in Sanskrit is called *santosha*. One of the nine guidelines for living in Patanjali's Yoga Sutras, santosha may seem like a strange concept. How often do we hear people say that they feel content? How often do you feel content? Have you ever felt content? Take a moment to think about the last time you felt content. Where were you? What were you doing? Why did that feeling leave you?

"Dwelling in the present moment, I know it is a beautiful moment." When you are truly present and allow yourself to experience life exactly the way it is, rather than how you think it should be, the miracle of the moment shines forth. The more you practice mindfulness, the more likely you are to appreciate the simple wonders of life on earth—a beautiful sunset, a cool breeze, the smile of a stranger, a hug from a loved one, a crisp apple. Rather than focusing on what we don't have, mindfulness encourages us to focus on what we do have. When we practice mindful breathing, we are continually reminded that we are alive, that we have this breath, and in this, we can be content. Isn't life itself the most fundamental thing we possess?

To practice contentment and find fulfillment in simple things are gifts to the living earth. "In a consumer society, contentment is a radical proposition," writes Robin Wall Kimmerer. "Recognizing abundance rather than scarcity undermines an economy that thrives by creating unmet desires. Gratitude cultivates an ethic of fullness, but the economy needs emptiness."[11] We have been told that we need material things to make us happy or to feel fulfilled, but this is not true. All you need to do is go camping for a week or two and you will soon realize that a roof over your head, a hot meal at the end of the day, a fire, and good company go a long way toward fostering a sense of contentment. The oceans on our planet today are choking with gyres the size of the state of Texas made of plastic garbage from our throw-away economy. Cultivating contentment through mindful engagement with the living earth can help us begin to make the shift to living more simply and transforming our economy from one that is anthrocentric to one that is ecocentric.

As a yoga teacher, I make a practice out of breathing with awareness every day. Over the years, this practice has become almost second nature. I find myself taking deep inhalations and complete exhalations at different points in the day to help me release stress and tension not only from my body but also from my awareness. I discovered early on that if I took a few moments to center my awareness through mindful breathing before heading into the forest for a hike, my experience in the forest changed dramatically. The breathing helped to quiet the activity of my mind, relax my body, and heighten my senses, while I maintained a state of alert relaxation. This is a key component in the outdoor experiences that I lead.

Inner-Space and Outer-Space Meditation

On your next outdoor adventure or quiet sit in your backyard, try the following exercise. Take a comfortable seat on the earth and lengthen your spine up through the crown of your head. Feel your sitz bones anchored firmly into the support of the earth and imagine that they are growing roots into the soil. Begin to slowly and consciously deepen your breath. Allow your eyes to close, and with each exhalation, let go of tension in the mind and body.

Next, begin to recite the following two phrases as you breathe in and out. With eyes closed, breathe in and say, *I feel my body,* and then with eyes opened, breathe out and say, *I feel the living earth.* Continue this cycle for a few minutes, noticing the flow of awareness traversing the boundary between your inner space and the space all around you.

When you have completed the exercise, rise and take a few minutes to walk with an awareness of your breath, or spend a few minutes journaling about the experience. Where is the boundary between your inner experience and the living earth? Has this boundary shifted or changed as a result of working with this meditation? If so, how?

Awake in the Forest

In this body, the mount Meru—i.e., the vertebral column—is surrounded by seven islands; there are rivers, seas, mountains, fields, and lords of the fields too. There are in it seers and sages; all the stars and planets as well. There are sacred pilgrimages, shrines, and presiding deities of the shrines. The sun and moon, agents of creation and destruction, also move in it. Ether, air, water, and earth are also there. All the beings that exist in the three worlds are also to be found in the body; surrounding the Meru, they are engaged in their respective functions. (But ordinary men do not know it.) He who knows all this is a Yogi; there is no doubt about it.   **SHIVA SAMHITA, 2.1**

Ancient schools of yoga sought to maximize a sense of aliveness through diet, exercise, attitude, and breathing practices. It was believed that yogic disciplines could help the yogi penetrate the depths of human consciousness and that the elemental forces that gave rise to all phenomena of the physical universe lay at the very foundation of consciousness itself. These schools saw the body as a sacred temple and believed that we could learn to live free as awakening human beings, liberated with wisdom and a greater capacity for goodness and purpose. Such people have reached a state known as *jivan mukti*, which means "liberated in life."

The fact that the yoga and the Buddhist traditions emerged from practitioners and monastic communities living in wild and often remote natural places tells us something about where we might go to find peace, wisdom, and a feeling of more aliveness. In my own experience, the awareness I have been able to cultivate through yoga has profoundly enhanced my connection to the living earth.

Living at the Kripalu Center as a young man, I practiced yoga three to four hours each day for a six-month period. It was a very special time in my life, one in which I was able to dive deep and focus on drawing close to myself in a safe and supportive environment. During that time, the mindfulness I was cultivating on my yoga mat and in my work as a volunteer dishwasher stayed with me when I wandered into the shadowed hemlock forest that borders the retreat center.

This land, watched over by towering, ancient trees and populated with moss-covered boulders, seemed to breathe and speak. As I walked mindfully out of the temperature-controlled environment of the retreat center and into the cold and refreshing winds of the winter woods, my senses were heightened. I experienced an almost overwhelming sense of awe for the power of the living earth, which seemed to flow around me and through me as I moved farther away from the retreat center's human activity and deeper into the forest's more-than-human world. The intensity and frequency of my yoga and mindfulness practices made me more sensitive to my embodied experience in the forest.

In my yoga practice, I was using *pranayama*, breathing practices, as well as *asana*, the yoga postures, to take my awareness into realms within the space of my own body, mind, and spirit. In yoga, turning inward and sensing inward is called *pratyahara*. Yogic tools are used to draw the mind's focus away from sensory objects and external desires and toward a state of alert and relaxed observation. With practice, they take us through a process of becoming sensitive to an inner field of knowing. I found that when I emerged from my inner journeys and headed out into the deep woods, my physical senses, now attuned to the subtle internal realms, were incredibly sensitive to what was swirling around me in the forest. I was, in fact, awake in the forest.

The loftiness of the ascending hemlock trunks, the bite of the cold wind, the smell of the pines, and the icy burn of the snow on my skin made it difficult for my mind to wander. In these moments, I felt intensely alive. As the months wore on, my sojourns into the lands around Kripalu continued, and as winter gave way gradually to spring, the land became lush and verdant. The hard, sharp ice became flowing water, the frozen earth became soft and aromatic, and the birds returned. What was an arctic world was now green, with misty clouds rising off the hills. The land was breathing again, and I with it.

We evolved in relationship with the ever-changing qualities of the seasons and landscapes, in relationship with trees, stones, mud, birds, antlers, claws, and teeth. Today, most of us live differently than our ancestors did, which is not wrong, but being sedentary and indoors most of the time isn't good for us. Many people think of the outdoors, of nature, as something other, something foreign and even frightening. Nature has become an abstraction, something out there rather than an extension of ourselves. Without the medicine of streams, forests, and other natural ecosystems, people turn to TV, food, alcohol, and other sedatives to fill an emptiness or to alleviate a boredom. With mindfulness, however, we can pierce the veil of abstraction, the filter of language, and the stories in our minds to directly experience the embodied nature of our right relationship with the earth. Mindfulness offers a way in, a tool to help people overcome their fears and reconnect with something deep, primal, and essential.

During a mindful outdoor experience I was leading on a winter solstice retreat in the forest near Kripalu, there was a woman who was not accustomed to navigating snow-covered, icy, and uneven terrain. While the group was gathered around a small fire, enjoying hemlock-needle tea, the woman came to me to say that she could not walk back the way we had come. It was too rugged, and she was frightened she would fall and hurt herself. I offered to walk back with her so she could make it back safely, and my assistant led the rest of the group ahead of us.

On our walk back, this woman and I got to talking, and it turned out she was writing a book about overcoming fear through mindfulness. As I guided her around the slickest parts of the trail, she held on to my elbow and shared that she was going to include this experience in her book. She realized that by using mindfulness, she could guide herself through the fear. It was a simple, everyday kind of experience, which you might not think of as rewilding, but for this woman, it was. She went beyond her comfort zone and made it through. Rewilding exists on a spectrum, and there are many points of entry for people who have different levels of comfort and familiarity with nature and the practice of mindfulness.

Natural Teachers

When we are disconnected from the living earth, we lose its life-affirming wisdom. In ancient India's *Ramayana*, the hero, Rama, who is an incarnation of Lord Vishnu (the sustainer of the Universe), is traveling through the forest with his younger brother, Lakshmana. Both have been unjustly exiled from their kingdom, even though Rama is the rightful heir to his family's throne. Rama's soul mate, Sita, has been taken prisoner by the demon king Ravana.

Lakshmana is very upset about all these injustices and is venting to his brother as they make their way through the dense and wild jungle, while Rama, who embodies patience, wisdom, and compassion, encourages his brother to let it go. They come to a pristine mountain lake and pause. The water is clear, cool, and clean. Rama dives into the water and floats out into the middle of the lake. Lakshmana asks his older brother, "Rama, how do you know when to take bold action against injustice and when to remain still and wait?" Rama answers, "When your mind is as cool and serene as this lake, my brother. Then you will know."

54

There was a time when more people had exposure to pristine lakes, open fields, mountains, little streams, boulders, and many of the other teachers who dwell in the more-than-human world. These manifestations of our living earth have been our friends, guides, and teachers for a long time, and evidence shows that exposure to such natural settings can be powerful buffers against stress for children and adults alike.[12] Yet today, more than half of the earth's population is urban dwelling. Most people use smartphones instead of the sun to tell time and instead of the moon for light at night. Rather than taking a walk outside and sitting under a tree when life gets us down, we post to Facebook, scroll through our news feed, or binge-watch Netflix. Perhaps we could use what author Richard Louv calls a little "vitamin N" (for nature). Like Rama, we can turn to the lakes, the sky, the earth, and the trees for guidance.

Cities by their very nature are the product of human thinking and expression. In a city, we are surrounded by buildings, roads, signs, stores, vehicles, and marketing campaigns that reflect back to us the cognitive processes of economic, political, and cultural agendas. The more-than-human world can also be found in cities. Hawks nest on tall buildings, and birds of all kinds live in small parks, gutters, trees, and abandoned buildings. In empty lots, insects and plants live, and squirrels, coyotes, foxes, and other wild creatures roam as well. Even in cities, the living earth bursts forth from every crack. So, we can engage in rewilding almost anywhere. The key is our intention, curiosity, and a willingness to look closely.

The more-than-human world is far more ancient than anything man-made. Its beings speak to us of timeless truths, and our consciousness opens to these old friends, as insights and emotions are unlocked in their presence and unfold for us. It is as if these environments hold the keys to our psyches. They help us let go of stress, remind us of our place in the universe, and show us the great cycles with which we are called to align ourselves.

Go and sit by a babbling brook and focus on the sound of the water. Listen to the sound of the wind. Gaze out over the ocean and listen to the rhythm of the water. Sit by a crackling fire and smell the aroma of smoke of dry pine branches popping as they release the stored light of the sun. Place your palms on warm concrete and feel the stable earth element beneath it supporting you. Ponder a dandelion growing nobly through a crack of concrete. Society may be telling us that we need more, always more, but stop and listen to what the earth and sky are trying to tell us. Take a deep breath and empty your mind as you exhale. Look around and receive the miracle of this moment. You are enough.

Ursasana: Bear Pose

> People say that what we're all seeking a meaning for life. I don't think that's what we're really seeking. I think that what we're seeking is an experience of being alive, so that our life experiences on the purely physical plane will have resonance with our own innermost being and reality, so that we actually feel the rapture of being alive.   JOSEPH CAMPBELL

Many years ago, a bear sat down next to me while I was meditating in the woods. It was an afternoon in mid-October in the Berkshires, and I had been mountain biking in my favorite preserve. I took a break from riding to enjoy the perfect fall afternoon. I was overflowing with gratitude. My life was going well.

I sat under a strong oak tree and closed my eyes. I asked Spirit to come and sit with me, to share in my heartfelt thanksgiving. I spoke the words aloud and immediately heard footsteps in the woods behind me. They got closer, but I continued with my meditation, until directly behind me, I heard a twig snap and a loud exhalation through a very big nose. I knew in that moment, in every cell of my body, that a bear was behind me.

My heart pounded, and adrenaline surged through my body. I was totally alert and aware. I very slowly turned my head to look behind me and saw shining black fur from shoulder to rump, close enough to reach out and touch. It was a large black bear. Immediately my mind provided options for survival. Get up and run away? Get up and yell to scare the bear away? Climb a tree? Those ideas seemed bad. Sit still, do nothing, and breathe? Yes, that made sense. And so I did. I slowed my breathing and meditated on the intensity of my body's response to this perceived threat.

In my yoga I had learned that strong sensations and emotions, including fear, can be powerful doorways into meditation. Rather than turning away from an uncomfortable experience, I had learned to breathe into what I was feeling. In this case, the fight-or-flight response was a huge wave washing over my mind, body, and soul. Instead of making a big story about what was happening, I remembered to face the experience in all of its raw power. I had the thought, *This is the coolest thing that has ever happened to me!* I had another thought, too: *This might be the worst thing that has ever happened to me!* Many hundreds of hours, I had practiced breathing through the intense sensations of yoga postures, watching my experience without reaction and allowing things to be the way they are. All that training on the mat was now being put to the test in a pose I had never tried before, Bear Pose, or *Ursasana.*

For a moment, I wondered how it might feel to be bitten by a bear. That was not a helpful thought, so I returned to my breathing. Moments seemed to stretch into hours. The bear walked out from behind the tree and sat next to me. It was smelling me. Still I remained motionless. In time, the bear walked away. I turned to look as it walked away. It turned to look back at me. Our eyes met, and then it disappeared down the hill. I stood up and fell down, my legs weak and wobbly. I stood again and got to my bike. I climbed on board and pedaled out of those woods like a bat out of hell!

For days, I was in a state of profound shock and elation. My life was filled with magic, possibility, and power. Anything could happen. I felt incredibly alive. The presence of the bear stayed with me—even to this day. I have never been a thrill seeker or adrenaline junkie. I've never jumped out of an airplane or tried bungee jumping. I've always been drawn to more meditative outdoor activities, like canoeing, archery, or watching birds. But sitting in meditation with a bear gave me an unexpected adrenaline jolt.

While sitting with a bear is not likely to happen to many people, you may encounter other life-forms or elements that can help you awaken and experience a greater degree of aliveness. We long for connection with our relatives who roam the forests and wild lands, and we still find nourishment in their company. In mindful rewilding, we open ourselves up to the sensations and life-giving experiences that the land holds for us. Such moments of communion between you and the living earth can open doorways into a more magical, mysterious, and meaningful life. And it makes all the difference to have the right mental tools and preparation to help you ride the waves of powerful energies you will encounter in both the human and the more-than-human worlds.

Skill in Action: Breathe, Relax, Feel, Watch, Allow

Yoga is skill in action.   BHAGAVAD GITA

Imagine if I had acted on my fear and allowed the adrenaline to make me react to the bear standing two feet behind me. What might have happened if I had jumped up suddenly and screamed or tried to climb a tree? What if you are having a challenging day at work and someone sends you an email that you find sharp, disrespectful, or unnecessary? Do you fire off the first reaction that comes to mind? Or do you pause, take a deep breath, and think about the ramifications?

There are times when an instinctive reaction is absolutely necessary, when you are in a life-threatening situation and have no time to reflect. Then the sympathetic nervous system takes control and helps you through it. Most of the time, however, our situations are not life-threatening, which means that reacting unthinkingly can often lead to outcomes that create more pain and suffering in the long run. This is why learning to pause and see the bigger picture can help us act more skillfully. Think about Edgar Mitchell looking down on this planet from outer space—that is what we are learning to do with mindfulness, except that the living earth is the experience we are seeing from a higher perspective, with a bigger view of time and the consequences of our actions.

In Kripalu Yoga, we have a method that helps us more skillfully navigate the strong sensations that arise in yoga practice. When held for long periods of time, yoga postures can generate powerful feelings. They were created to help us move through and release any energy blocks in our minds and bodies, places where stress or life experience has caused us to tense up and armor ourselves. These postures also help us when we encounter the discomfort that direct contact with the living earth can bring, such as experiences of cold, wet rain, mosquitos, or oppressive heat and humidity. When sitting with that bear, I used a technique we lovingly call "BRFWA": Breathe, Relax, Feel, Watch, Allow.

You might use BRFWA on your first walk in a park or a wood that is new to you. You might use it during your first solo camping experience or when you see an animal that frightens you. I once used BRFWA when I got caught in a rip current while swimming off the Big Island of Hawaii. It allowed me to remain calm and to act skillfully, possibly saving my life. In any survival situation, the first advice is almost always to remain calm and think, not to react or panic. But how we are supposed to do that is not often explained.

By practicing mindful rewilding, you are not looking to put yourself in a survival situation, though many of these skills can help you feel more confident and capable when you're away from the conveniences of modern society. Inevitably, the more time we spend outdoors, the more likely we are to come up against our comfort zone or find ourselves in a situation where remaining calm and being skillful are necessary. In these moments, BRFWA can be a great ally.

I recommend that you use BRFWA regularly as a moment-to-moment practice. Using it daily will support you developing a general state of mindfulness. You can also use BRFWA to go deeper into a pleasant experience. Maybe you practice it when you take a walk or when you dip your feet in a cool stream or when you feel a fresh breeze moving through your neighborhood. Practice BRFWA regularly so that when something truly challenging happens, it is second nature for you, as it was for me when I had my encounters with the bear and the rip current.

BRFWA: Breathe, Relax, Feel, Watch, Allow

To begin working with BRFWA outdoors, try the following steps.

1. **Go outside.** Find a place where you can sit comfortably and have a view of a natural, outdoor space. (This might also be the place where you want to establish your daily nature meditation.)

2. **Get grounded.** Feel your sitz bones and imagine they are plugging in to the earth. As you ground down through your seat, also lengthen your spine and let it rise up through the crown of your head. Imagine that your spine is the trunk of a great tree and you are the bridge that connects the heavens and the earth.

3. **Breathe.** Soften your belly, and slowly deepen your breathing with each inhalation and exhalation. If possible, breathe in and out through the nose. A good ratio for this breath is to inhale for four counts and hold the breath gently for seven counts; then exhale for eight counts, and repeat the cycle. As you breathe, notice the qualities of the air. What is the temperature? Is it hot, cold, or somewhere in between? How moist or dry is the air? What can you smell? Leaves, pine needles, the smoke from nearby fireplaces? In which direction is the wind moving? What can you hear? Your breath, your heartbeat, your joints settling? Branches creaking against each other, leaves rustling in the breeze, dew dripping to the ground, chipmunks

or squirrels scampering, crows cawing, pigeons cooing, an airplane passing overhead?

4. **Relax.** As you breathe, begin to consciously scan your body. Notice any places where you are holding tension. Focus on each of these places, as you continue to breathe calmly and deeply, and invite these places to soften and let go. Maybe your forehead is tense, and your brow is furrowed. Maybe your shoulders are tight and raised with tension. Perhaps your jaw is clenched. See if you can allow your jaw to relax, so that your teeth are parted. Invite your tongue to sit heavy and relaxed in your mouth, with the tip of the tongue resting against the ridge of skin behind your two front top teeth. With each exhalation, feel tension melting out of your body, mind, and spirit. Relax into the support of the earth element. Feel the earth beneath you and within your bones and muscles.

5. **Feel.** As you continue to breathe and relax, notice what you can feel. Notice your body and what your body can feel—the air on your skin, the earth against your buttocks and legs, the light on your skin or coming through your clothing. Notice your heart and how you are feeling right now, not from a place of judgment, but from a place of compassion for yourself, and from a larger perspective, from your witness. Notice how the breath moving in and out helps you to feel more. This is one of the great secrets of yoga: the more deeply you breathe, the more of your own life you can feel.

6. **Watch.** Be the witness. Observe your experience and allow as much space as you can for whatever

is happening to be the way it is. Simply observe the land around you. Notice movement wherever it may be. Watch the play of light and the subtle movement created by the atmosphere's constant state of motion. Watch everything, and be curious about any life you see, whether birds in the bushes or trees, ants crawling on the ground, or a squirrel leaping from limb to limb. When you come into the present moment using these steps, doors of perception will open to you. You will see the world through new eyes.

7. **Allow.** Let it be. Let the moment be exactly the way that it is. Let go of grasping to your idea of what this moment should be. Let go of any aversion to things as they are. See if you can simply allow this moment to be as it is, and give yourself the opportunity to experience this moment right now in its pure expression. No matter the weather, no matter the terrain, can you allow this living earth and your relationship with it to be the way that it is? Moment by moment, can you keep letting go of your opinions, preferences, and judgments? It's not easy for any of us, which is why we practice. This awareness is something to come back to moment after moment after moment, always beginning again.

Moving from the human world, which is often fast-paced and frenetic, into the rhythms and cycles of the living earth is an adjustment. Our modern world is dramatically out of sync with the pace of nature, and even people who enjoy being outdoors don't always take the time to meet nature where it is. But when we are centered and in a mindful state of being, we are more closely attuned to the presence, cadence, and language of the living earth. We can leave our troubles at the trailhead, exhaling and letting go of any agenda we might be carrying, simply allowing the land to hold us for a time.

When we invite mindfulness in nature, we draw our awareness closer to the wilderness-dwelling spiritual seekers and communities who journey into the higher realms of consciousness. When we inhabit the present moment, we draw closer as well to our wild relatives in the branches, burrows, bushes, and other folded contours in this living earth. With our bare feet on the ground and our breath flowing steady and smooth, we become steady both in our inner and outer landscape.

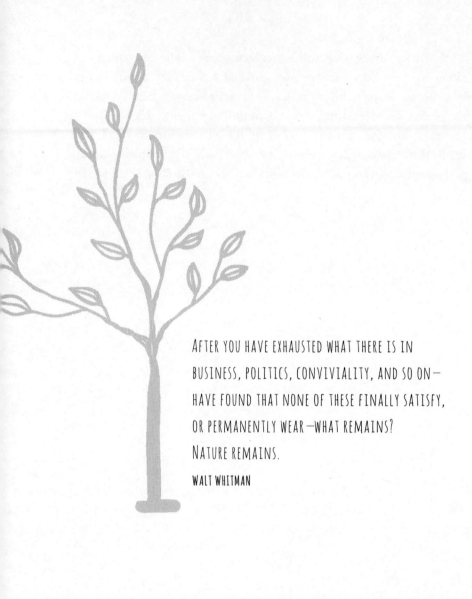

After you have exhausted what there is in
business, politics, conviviality, and so on—
have found that none of these finally satisfy,
or permanently wear—what remains?
Nature remains.

WALT WHITMAN

3

THE LIVING EARTH

Paths to Your Wildness

Cultural historian Thomas Berry says, "Walt Whitman did not invent his sentience, nor was he wholly responsible for the form of feelings he experienced. Rather, his sentience is an intricate creation of the Milky Way, and his feelings are an evocation of being, an evocation involving thunderstorms, sunlight, grass, history and death. Walt Whitman is a space the Milky Way fashioned to feel its own grandeur."[1]

Let me repeat that last sentence, "Walt Whitman is a space the Milky Way fashioned to feel its own grandeur." And so, I believe, are you and I.

You have a capacity for beholding the wonder of life on earth, and when you do that, you allow the universe to contemplate itself through you. The challenge for most people is learning how to befriend the mind so that day-to-day worries, stresses, and other thoughts we carry around don't get in the way of experiencing the miracle of life on earth. It's not that thoughts are bad or that forethought, planning, and strategic thinking aren't useful; they are. We wouldn't be here without them. But we need to be able to put them aside regularly in order to return to the present moment and to the earth and to ourselves through the body and the senses as well as the mind.

The practice of meditation is the most powerful tool for developing the capacity to calm the fluctuations of our thoughts. Of course, just by spending time close to nature, our physiology knows how to attune with the forces of the earth, so much of the work of rewilding has to do with slowing down and falling into rhythm with nature.

Have you ever been spellbound by the beauty of some simple thing in nature? Maybe the specks of dust caught in a ray of light coming through your window, their dance and the angle of the light casting radiance all about you, transforming what seemed an ordinary moment into something else, magical, sacred, maybe. Each of us has the ability to open our senses and experience the beauty and wonder of this life. We are the stewards of this garden. Our species can create and destroy on a grand scale. Like a drop of dew, our consciousness can open itself to the vastness of a million universes, or it can close itself to just our little world. It's up to us.

Stepping out of doors and into the moving air, where the sounds, smells, sights, textures, and other subtle messages of the more-than-human world are moving, activates our ancient, "wilder" selves. Outside, we have access to more life force, the *prana* of yoga. Think of life force simply as the presence of living things and their energy, their chemistry, electrical charge, and the electromagnetic fields around them. How much more life is present in a field or forest than in your living room or an office or in a department store? How is the quality of the air different in these places? Where do you tend to feel more alive? How do you feel when you head into a forest, where myriad life-forms live in a dynamic environment and present an abundance of sensory information to absorb?

Rewilding is a journey of discovery, where we use natural vehicles to take us to places that will expand our awareness and experience of being alive on this earth and in this body. Perhaps your connection with nature is a tree you climb, a boulder where you take your seat, or a stream that bathes you in liquid and sound. Perhaps you allow your eyes, ears, and skin to come into relationship with the heat, flames, and sounds of a fire as you meditate on the enchanting light—the occasional pop calling you back from your mind's wandering and into the living night.

Different sections in this chapter provide ways to stimulate your mind and senses and more fully experience your embodied awareness outdoors.

The consciousness we bring to anything is the single most powerful determinant of our experience. If we approach the earth with fear or a desire for conquest, our experience will be profoundly different than if we approach with reverence and respect and a desire to care and coexist.

Interbeing

> If you are a poet, you will see clearly that there is a cloud floating in this sheet of paper. Without a cloud, there will be no rain; without rain, the trees cannot grow; and without trees, we cannot make paper. The cloud is essential for the paper to exist. If the cloud is not here, the sheet of paper cannot be here either. So, we can say that the cloud and the paper inter-are.   THICH NHAT HANH

I don't know about you, but I find it easy to slip into a way of being in which I feel separated from everything. My clothes, my house, my job, my family; all of these "I, me, mines" reinforce an idea that I am something distinct from the rest of the universe. In fact, most people spend their lives building this sense of self, like building a real-life bitmoji, first establishing its character and then spending their lives defending and supporting the story of that character. Inevitably, though, life wins. No matter how much we try to protect our fragile sense of self, greater forces will have their way and break down what is made up.

Modern societies like to pretend we can isolate and separate ourselves from nature, and many aim to insulate themselves from the earth, to create a permanent disconnect between our bodies and our Mother's touch. Most children learn to walk with rubber-soled sneakers before their toes ever know the soil or grass, pebbles, mud, or sand. Ticks, mosquitoes, and poison ivy become the boogeymen of the forest, and hypersanitized indoor spaces are where many people now feel most at home. When we can seal ourselves indoors, eating food in sealed packages, drinking water from sealed bottles, ingesting prepackaged information, even breathing air filtered through air conditioners, we can easily think that this is the way things really are.

But, of course, this is not the way things really are. Our bodies were not grown in petri dishes but evolved out of the living earth, a part of all that is. We share our cells and the air in our lungs with all of life. The pollution we put into our atmosphere we put into ourselves. Remember that the air we breathe today was on the other side of the planet just a few days ago, exhaled by trees and the ocean. In this way, these great characters of nature live within us, and they exist in relationship with us. Our existence interpenetrates. As Thay says, we "inter-are."

The word *universe* is made up of two separate terms, "uni," meaning "one," and "verse," which means "song." Our universe is "one song." Everything that exists is vibrating to the tune of creation, and we are a part of that great music that is playing and being played through us and all that is.

When we invite our awareness to rest in the present moment, we can clearly sense that the way of everything *is* in a state of interbeing. This knowledge that all of life is connected lies at the root of many spiritual and mystical traditions. It stirs our souls, lifts our awareness above the fear and struggle of our individual existence, and places us in a much larger whole, part of the great mystery. What if you could connect with this lofty way of being every day? How would your life be different? What might you do differently? Spending mindful time outdoors, entering into relationship with the forces and manifestations of the earth, is a powerful doorway to the awareness of interbeing.

During a five-day mindfulness immersion in the winter woods at Kripalu, we spent at least five hours outside every day. We navigated over frozen streams and stood under huge trees, as the wind blew fresh snow down from the boughs and onto our upturned faces. We tracked fox, coyote, white-footed mice, and fishers. One of the students in the program was quite tall and imposing, yet out on the trail, he was surprisingly unsteady. He seemed out of his element. After a few days, he shared with the group that in his normal life he spends 95 percent of his waking hours sitting behind a computer. When he isn't at a screen, he's reflecting on how he could have done a better job at work or preparing to go back to work. "I feel so disconnected from reality," he said. He was not only disconnected from other people and the natural world but also from his own body and self. But after a few days in the awe-inspiring winter woods, with ample time for reflection, encouragement to breathe deeply, and a community of kind people, this hardworking man began to reconnect with his embodied experience of life.

Interbeing

Take yourself to a place you enjoy in nature, or look out a window onto a green space or other natural setting. Stand or sit comfortably, with your feet anchored into the support of the earth. Gently lengthen your spine up through the crown of your head, as if your spine just grew an inch or two longer. Draw a soft breath in through your nose and hold it in for a moment, then exhale slowly and allow your shoulders and abdomen to relax as you follow your breath all the way out. Take a deep breath in and exhale through your mouth with a gentle sigh or sound. Soften your face and relax your jaw; allow your teeth to part slightly and your eyes to rest like big pools in their sockets. Let go.

Watch the little pulse of movement in your belly as the body breathes on its own. Stay with your breath and notice the activity of your mind. Feel the breath entering your body, and feel the breath leaving your body. The atmosphere of the planet is moving in and out of you. Each exhalation is inhaled by another being, perhaps by a tree. Each inhalation was exhaled by other beings, trees, and oceans. This breath, has been recycled on our planet for hundreds of millions of years. This breath, right now, so ancient, yet so fresh.

If you'd like, take a walk as you stay with your breath. If your attention wanders into thinking, come back to the anchor of your breath. Look around, take in your surroundings. Notice the way that life is connected. The bird, connected to the air, rides on currents of atmosphere. The puddle holds the water that cycles through us all. The material for your clothes was grown on farmland. The cotton blossomed under our only sun, was watered by passing clouds, then harvested and spun and woven and delivered by other humans until its destination in this moment with this body. Notice how things are connected, how they "inter-are."

How might you bring this way of seeing with you to your life indoors, at work and at home?

Whenever you are in your "normal life" and things get stressful or you feel disconnected from the web of life, try pausing to remember a restorative time you spent outdoors. Close your eyes and take a soft breath in and a long breath out. Just remembering the sound of wind in the trees can help to center and calm you. Remember that nature is not an abstract place outside of you—you are a part of nature. You are an imaginative and self-aware expression of the creative life force in this uni-verse. One song.

Animacy

Language is powerful. The words we use and the concepts we choose to contain our life experience shape how we think about and experience reality, so our language has profound impacts. The most common word I hear to describe all that is of the earth and outside the realm of human invention is *nature*. The term is used to speak about forests, mountains, oceans, and any part of our earth that has not been totally burned, bulldozed, paved, or built on. Animals and plants, weather, geology, and ecology all fall within nature. In fact, nature seems to include almost everything except human beings and the things we create. Yet we too are an expression of nature.

Life evolved out of the primordial oceans, from single-celled organisms to complex beings, including the 37 trillion-celled, self-aware animals that we are today. From that perspective, you and I are part of the consciousness of the earth itself. We are part of this planet and supported by it. So, to me, the word *nature* alone doesn't convey our true state of interbeing. By now, I'm sure you've noticed that I use the terms "the living earth" and "the more-than-human world" in place of *nature*.

As you draw closer to the living earth, this perspective can help you break through limited ways of relating to the more-than-human world and provide insights that bridge the chasm formed between us and the land we live on. We may be domesticated, but we can take small steps to find our inner wild selves, and in so doing, bring a more balanced human consciousness back into relationship with our many relations on this planet, including paw, wing, fin, wind, and the rest.

> The old Lakota was wise, he knew that man's
> heart away from nature becomes cold and hard,
> and that a lack of respect for green, growing
> things soon leads to a lack of respect for people
> too.   LUTHER STANDING BEAR[2]

My yoga teacher trainer, Yoganand, often says that after a deep relaxation at the end of a yoga class, he goes outside and sees the trees and the mountains and notices that they are not the same trees and mountains that he saw before class. They are more vibrant, vivid, emanating a life presence that he missed somehow before the class. What changed? Was it the earth, or was it his perception?

One day in late October in the Berkshires, I was taking a yoga training that involved breathing techniques and internal disciplines intended to increase the flow of *prana*. After a full morning of practice,

I went outside to get some fresh air. It was unusually warm for the time of year, with temperatures in the mid-80s. The sun was shining, the air was dry, and a steady wind was blowing out of the south. The leaves on a favorite sugar maple were swooshing as I'd never before seen. The tree was talking up a storm! I sat in the grass and stared at that tree for over an hour, transfixed by its character, its beauty, and its sheer aliveness. Ever since that day, the tree and I have a bond. I would even go so far as to call it a friendship.

Certain spiritual practices shift our attention from the thinking to the feeling mind. Rather than projecting a limited concept onto the sugar maple, naming it, and assigning to it a list of categories before moving on, I experienced the maple in its present moment of self-expression. It wasn't only a tree—it was color, texture, motion, sound, joy, and memories of autumns long gone. The tree was a living being, with a personality, character, and presence. Sitting for hours in meditation, watching stories and thoughts float across the movie screen of my mind, and breathing until my body vibrates with presence, changes me. It means that when I walk outdoors, everything I see reflects back to me my ability to perceive, feel, and sense life. The tree didn't change; I changed. The lens of my perception had been cleaned up a little, so my view on the world widened, deepened, and came into sharper focus. This heightened state of awareness promotes our making connections with people and places. These connections nourish us, but we can make them only when we are present.

REANIMATING

Go outside and find a nice place to sit. Close your eyes and begin to deepen your breath. As you breathe in, feel the sensations of breathing in. As you breathe out, feel the sensations of breathing out. Continue to breathe with this awareness for five minutes or so. When you take a final deep breath in, let it out with a gentle sigh or a soft sound. Now, notice what sounds you can hear. Notice the light coming through your closed eyelids. As you are ready, slowly open your eyes. Allow the light of the world to enter into your awareness and give yourself permission to simply observe your world. Let go of needing to put any names or labels on anything; just look out and take it all in. After five minutes or so, get up and walk mindfully, feeling each step and imagining that you are sending gratitude to the earth that supports you. Enjoy this time to simply be and receive the beauty of the earth. You can conclude this practice with a few minutes of journaling or sketching. Whatever you do, enjoy this time to simply be and receive the beauty of the earth.

Many children have had a bond with a tree or a stone or other natural being. As we grow up, however, we are taught that rocks and trees are objects, things, not people like us. We learn to see them as resources that exist for our own needs. Trees are the wood that make baseball bats, and rocks are pulverized to make building materials. We even learn to see animals as objects. We refer to them not as "they" or "them" but as "it." "Hey, there's a fox over there!" "Where? I don't see *it*."

Many indigenous cultures refer to the more-than-human worlds as people. Clouds, trees, stones, plants, all belong to their own community, speak their own language, and have their own relationship to the spirit that moves through all things. The first time I recognized these more-than-human communities and felt their presence strongly as an adult was when I had spent a lot of time in the woods and became fascinated with trees. I noticed that in some places, many American beech trees grew together, while in other places, eastern hemlock congregated. In the beech groves, the simple-toothed leaves quaked in the breeze; their smooth, grey trunks reminded me of the mallorn trees from *The Lord of the Rings*. I couldn't help but feel the presence of elves in those beech groves!

In the hemlock groves, the shadows were deep, and the earth moist. The deep green boughs stretched and gently bobbed on the breeze, light, buoyant, and mysterious. The hemlock groves were hushed. Silence and watchfulness permeated the hemlocks' shadows. Families of white pine created sun-toasted auburn carpets of needles, soft and aromatic in the afternoon light. Their trunks climbed high into the sky, and their bluish-green pine needles shone bright and happy in the sun. A feeling of optimism and joy seemed to ring out when white pine needles shimmered in the sunlight. Under these mighty trees were perfect places to lie down or to sit and lean against trunks, perfect places to take in the tranquility of the land.

Looking into the distance, I could see patches of forest green on mountain slopes where communities of evergreens lived, and then the grey patches in the fall from oaks and maples that had lost their leaves. Suddenly it hit me: these are communities, tribes, families. Before this, I had not really seen or felt the profound reality of community that exists among trees of the same species, trees that congregate. Now, when I look out at hills or mountains in the distance, I see the tribes of tree beings whose presence creates a tapestry of color and texture all across our forested lands.

Trees communicate and support one another. Forest ecology expert Peter Wohlleben refers to the nutrient and information exchange that exists among trees in the microbial network underground as the "wood wide web."[3] There is evidence that trees work together to keep elder trees alive and that they warn one another of danger. We are symbionts with trees, relying on the oxygen they provide while they rely on the carbon dioxide we exhale. There is a give and take, a reciprocity, that binds us to the trees, plants, and other members of our earth community, all of whom share the atmosphere, nutrients, and waters of this living earth. To think of trees as objects denies what they are. To think that way minimizes and flattens the complex and mysterious reality of their "treeness." This objectification of the living earth, whether it be trees, minerals, or animals, also flattens our consciousness and experience, causing us to miss out on so much of the beauty, love, and wonder to be found in relationship with the earth. When we think of the earth as composed of so many lifeless objects, we give ourselves permission to treat them as such. If we take the time to slow down, to be mindful and observe the land, trees, and other crewmates of spaceship Earth, we strengthen our ability to see the reality of life's living connections.

Reciprocity

> Keep close to Nature's heart . . . and break clear away, once in a while, and climb a mountain or spend a week in the woods. Wash your spirit clean.   JOHN MUIR

Rewilding is a way of seeing and being in relationship to life, and it can include learning ancestral skills for survival. Tom Brown Jr., a great tracking teacher I noted earlier in the book, emphasizes the profound role gratitude and thanksgiving played in what he learned from his teacher Stalking Wolf, a Lipan Apache tracker and spiritual teacher. To truly feel and connect with the miracle of any living thing, any gift of the Creator, whether a piece of wood being carved into a sacred pipe or a plant or animal being harvested for food, one must honor the other being's sacrifice and give thanks for what is received from that being. All of life is an exchange of energy. To live, all living things must consume, and in turn, be consumed. There is no escaping this.

> Of all the world's wonders, which is the most wonderful? That no man, though he sees others dying all around him, believes that he himself will die.   YUDHISHTARA

To be awake to the wonder of life is to be in a state of constant thanksgiving, for this breath, this bite of food, this caress of wind, this sunset, this chance to grow and serve others. A society whose people are involved in harvesting their food from their environment will likely be a culture that appreciates and that values thanksgiving. I believe that our collective loss of reverence for nature is in part due to our disconnect from the origin of our food. Pulling a potato or carrot out of the soil provides a sensual, embodied experience of taking life.

When we take life, we have a natural inclination to want to give back, to restore balance.

We all need to embrace the ethic of thanksgiving again so that we don't take the biodiversity of earth for granted. We can't pretend that the water and air we pollute aren't the water and air we rely on for our survival, for our health and well-being. A great start for a thanksgiving practice is with the breath, the thing we rely on most and most immediately. The birds who fly in the sky fly on our very breath. The air sweeps all around us, moving clouds, bringing snow and rain, making waves, and flowing in and out of our bodies with the oxygen that allows us to exist. The air we breathe moves the leaves in the trees, creating beautiful sounds that soothe our souls. We can go weeks without food and days without water but only a couple of minutes without the gift of breath. Throughout the world, there are cultures that hold the air and the wind as holy, as life-giving forces. The entire yoga tradition revolves around the fundamentals of breath, which can unlock expanded states of awareness and foster deep insights.

Here is a simple breathing practice you can work with to calm the nervous system, open to the senses, and become present to what is happening.

THE LONG EXHALE

When you are outside and about to begin a time of mindfulness, invite a slow, deep breath into your lungs through the nose. Hold the breath for a second or two before you exhale, and then exhale slowly through the mouth so that your exhalation is about twice as long as your inhalation. Repeat this breath at least four times. Your eyes can be open or closed, whichever feels better for you in the moment. In whatever direction you focus, internal or external, focus on the sensations and actions of the breath that is flowing in and out of you. When your mind wanders, come back to the breath and let it root you in the now.

This practice will help you get out of your thinking mind and into your feeling body. It will help you be present for what is happening in the moment. As you spend more time outdoors, the teachings of the earth will begin to show themselves to you. Ants, spiders, trees, and stones can be great teachers when we allow ourselves the curiosity and presence to open to what they have to share.

Giving Thanks

When I exhale, I know that the carbon dioxide flowing out of me will be absorbed by plant life and that the oxygen the plants exhale will flow into me. In my lifetime, I will ingest many living things, fruits, vegetables, animals, and water, and one day my body will return to the earth, and other living things will eat me.

We are only stewards of our bodies for a time. Every seven or so years, every molecule in this body will have been replaced, so that the me I think of as me is stable only in my mind. Who I really am is living in a dynamic state of reciprocity with the cosmos. Our planet, which includes us, is made up of elements generated in ancient star explosions. So, when we walk barefoot in the grass, stand at the entrance to a forest, or look up at the cool moon on an autumn evening, we can acknowledge that we are not simply receiving beauty from a heavenly body, that there is more going on. Through mindfulness we can hold an awareness of our situation, one in which we are suspended between using and being used, between eating and being eaten, between enjoying and being enjoyed.

When did people stop talking to the earth? How does one thank the moon for being all that the moon is? I've made a habit of speaking to trees, stones, salamanders, the wind, and any other relative I see outside. I speak to everything in nature. Why? When I speak to the forest, it feels as if my words are resonating not only in the cavities of my human body but also through the air, back into my eardrums, and bouncing on trees, leaves, and stones. When spoken from the heart to the living earth, my words express love for what I experience as my greater self. I know that hemlocks and stones do not understand the English language; I am not anthropomorphizing them. Yet I feel fuller and more connected when I give myself permission to speak to the land. When I converse with the earth, sometimes the wind blows suddenly, as if in response, or a squirrel will throw a pine cone out of a tree, which also feels like some kind of answer. I don't think we need to feel so isolated on this earth, so cut off and separate. We can honor our reciprocity with all of life by opening up the channels of communication with the more-than-human world.

Giving Thanks

The next time you experience a perfect sunset, a refreshing walk through new fallen snow, or the gift of seeing a wild animal, consider offering a gesture of gratitude to the living earth. Drawing your hands to prayer in front of the heart and bowing to the light in that manifestation of the universe, you can simply say "thank you." You might offer a small token, such as an acorn, a pine cone, crystal, or small pebble, to show your thanks. You could also make an earth mandala, creating a circular symbol with natural objects you gather, and offer it with gratitude. As the days and months go by, the mandala will be received into the earth. You could also take a handful of water from a pond, lake, stream, bay, or ocean and speak your words of love and gratitude into the water, allowing your prayer to slip through your fingers and become one with the water of the earth. Maybe you would like to burn a locally and sustainably harvested ceremonial incense such as cedar or mugwort, placing your intentions in the burning ember so that the rising smoke carries your prayer of gratitude and love to the heavens. These are small gestures, but they are powerful. These actions build a habit of focusing on the many ways we are in a deep state of interbeing with all of creation.

Noticing and Thanking

The next time you're outside, take a few soft breaths until you feel calm and centered in yourself. Take a look around and notice everything. Listen to the earth. Feel the air on your skin and in your lungs. Sense the support of the land holding you up and the force of gravity grounding you. Reflect on the mystery of life. How did this living earth emerge from the dark vacuum of space? How did everything evolve to be just as it is? What are the chances? In this moment, as you receive yet another breath from the invisible element of air, consider to what you owe your life in this living earth. What do you require to live? What essential ingredients do you receive each day and each moment that allow you to stay alive? What needs are being met that allow you to sit here with a living body? Breathe into that. Then, if you feel called, express your gratitude in any way that feels good to you. Maybe whisper "thank you" to the sky, or touch the earth and say a prayer. Let your bare feet feel the earth, and send loving kindness down into the soil. Whatever you do, let it be your true prayer. Don't ask for anything; only say thank you.

Species Connection and Biophilia

> One should pay attention to even the smallest crawling creature for these too may have a valuable lesson to teach us, and even the smallest ant may wish to communicate to a man. BLACK ELK

According to the Anxiety and Depression Association of America, 40 million Americans are afflicted with an anxiety disorder.[4] What if part of the great sadness upon our species comes from our separation from all the other species that are our relatives, from our separation from the living earth? Haven't we been separated from our family members, the bears and wolves, the butterflies and frogs, and the eagles and whales, to name just a few? Although many people are brought up to relate to animals as things, as creatures beneath us, humans feel an affinity, or biophilia, for other animals.[5] Animals may not feel all of the feelings we feel, but they certainly share in much of what it is to be alive on this earth. They have access to their senses and ways of experiencing life that we do not. Our many relatives are not exactly like us, but to diminish them because they are not like us is to overlook their uniqueness and overstate the superiority we think we possess. Animals have skills we do not have, whether the freedom to soar and see above it all, to burrow and live in the belly of the earth, to call to the moon in a pack, or to sing great songs from the ocean's depths.

What are we missing when we are apart from nature? What feelings are not being stirred that only a hawk's shrill cry or a buck's antlers in the morning mist can awaken? How impoverished have we become, locking ourselves in square rooms, away from the sound of wind, the light of stars, and the presence of the more-than-human world?

To connect with our wild selves, we need to reach out to the rest of nature and close up the distance, in physical space and in our hearts and minds. We don't need to walk in grizzly country or go on safari to do this. We can do it by opening ourselves to little things, things we might take for granted, like the robins in our backyard, the ladybug inside our window, the seagull on the beach, or the salamander we see on the path in the forest.

Imagine you just landed on earth from another planet. What a wonder each life-form would be! Imagine how exotic it would seem to you and how curious you would be about everything you see and experience. In the language of Zen Buddhism, this way of perceiving is called beginner's mind. Every life-form on earth is unique and has its own medicine, its own wisdom to share, if we make the time to be interested.

Just before my first child was born, I spent a lot of time walking along the banks of the Housatonic River in the Berkshires. One late summer afternoon, while exploring a flood plain near the banks, I came upon the skull of an animal, perfectly preserved on top of flattened old grasses. I stooped down to examine it. The skull was about the size of my palm, with two curving teeth protruding just below the nasal cavity. It was the skull of a young beaver. Beavers are well known for their hard work and ingenuity. After some time to appreciate the skull for the gift it was and reflecting on the qualities of the beaver, I also took it as a sign that a time of hard work was ahead of me—and it did indeed prove so. I became a father and my professional career took off. The beaver inspired me to do what needed to be done for my growing family.

Deep in a hemlock forest is a gurgling stream I like to bring people to. It has plenty of good stones, old stones for sitting and listening to the language of water. Sometimes when we sit near a certain pool on the edge of the brook, a small green frog comes out to sit with us. Students have remarked that sitting with the frog during the water meditation is deeply moving. This simple and unintimidating encounter with a frog provides a connection and a respite from species loneliness. One being with another, simply sitting and enjoying the same afternoon together.

Take some time right now to reflect on your connection with other nonhuman life-forms on this earth. What would it look like and what would it feel like to invite a rekindling of your relationships with other species? What calls out to you? Are there small actions you can start with?

Here are a few options:

- **Bird Watching.** In urban and suburban areas, bird watching is a great way to reconnect with the more-than-human world.

As David Lindo, better known as the Urban Birder, reminds us, "Look up!" This gives you a broader perspective immediately, and you will be surprised by the birds that frequently appear in pocket parks, tree-lined streets, yards, and gardens. You'll also notice the sky, the clouds, wind, and weather and appreciate them more. Today, birdwatchers are becoming younger, more urban, and more diverse, and they're also connecting with each other and advocating to protect the earth and its species.

- **Nature Meditation.** There is no substitute for sitting outside every day and getting to know the creatures you share the land with around your home. After sitting quietly for a few minutes, birds and other animals may appear and go about their business around you. Some people have actually befriended chickadees and hummingbirds, who eat or drink from their hands.

- **Cat or Dog Rescue.** Adopting a cat or a dog allows you to have a relationship with another species that can be profound. Animals experience the world differently. Observing them and interacting with them, we broaden our senses and awareness.

- **Wildlife Photography.** Place a trail camera on a tree near your home. You may catch a glimpse of a hidden world outside your door. You will become more aware of and connected to other beings you share the land with.

Topophilia

Rewilding allows you to see your environment with new eyes, sometimes as if for the very first time. You become more intimate with all its life-forms and sometimes see beyond the visible, connecting with a greater spirit, or presence. In his book *The Nature Principle*,

Richard Louv discusses "place blindness," which afflicts people who live so much of their lives indoors or in front of screens that they do not look up to see the land they live on. As with a psychological state such as inattentional blindness or perceptual blindness, these people do not perceive what is right in front of them, whether that is a horizon, a rock, a landscape, or a tree. Whether they are overwhelmed, overstressed, or preoccupied by other stimuli, in effect, they become sealed off from the elements, the seasons, and the real world of the living earth, and they lose out on the benefits of a vibrant and reciprocal relationship with nature.

Because place blindness inevitably leads to a disconnection with the living earth, it also leads to a lack of caring and interest in the planet's well-being. Future generations will not value and care for the earth if they have little or no actual relationship with it. People will not work to reverse climate change if they are so rarely outside that they have no embodied experience of its reality.

So how do we overcome place blindness? We embrace mindfulness and take it outside with us. The more time we spend out on the land, exploring and learning about the different plants and animals, the natural history and ecology, and simply enjoying and getting to know the contours of the living earth, the more bonded we'll feel to the places we call home. The more intimate we become with the land, the more we'll grow to love and cherish it. The word *land* can be a vague, general term, but as you get to know a place, you discover its individuality, its individual trees, stones, birds, and landmarks. Walking along a favorite trail as the months and years go by, I watch little saplings grow. As you walk, I encourage you to bring your full, penetrating awareness to the reality of life as it is. This kind of intimacy with place is as natural as can be. We've lost it only in the last hundred or so years. But we can get it back and be enriched again.

Some call this love of land *topophilia*. Every spot on a map has a unique quality and personality. Bioregionalism is a movement that seeks to understand the watersheds, geography, ecology, natural history, human history, and other layers of knowledge that make up the richness of a place. Climate change compels us to become more bioregional so that we can address some of the nasty repercussions of a society crumbling under the compounding costs of extreme weather events, food production problems, mass migrations, rampant pollution, and social strife. Stewardship begins with you and me.

Overcoming Place Blindness

- **Walk outside.** Whether you live in a populated neighborhood or in a more isolated area, walk outside every day. While you walk, open your senses, connect with your breath, and pay attention to movement on the land and in the sky.

- **Become an amateur naturalist.** Learn about the trees, plants, animals, insects, and other features of the land where you live. Use field guides to learn what trees grow near your home. Learn about the wild edibles that grow near you. Pay attention to the birds. Are there watersheds nearby? Where does the water flow from? Where does it flow to?

- **Join local organizations that support the land.** Make friends with local conservation, land management, and other environmental organizations that are active in your area. Perhaps there are walking or hiking groups, foraging clubs, craftspeople, or other groups you can learn and explore with.

- **Limit your screen time.** When you are outdoors, set a strong intention to experience the earth directly through your own senses. Silence your phone and put it away. Resist the urge to capture everything with a picture and instead take mental pictures of what you see. Practice letting go of the need to document every scene. See if you can reconnect with what it is like to experience life. Slow down and notice, as if for the very first time.

Waking Your Senses

> Owning up to being an animal, a creature of the
> earth. Tuning our animal senses to the sensible terrain:
> blending our skin with the rain-rippled surface of rivers,
> mingling our ears with the thunder and the thrumming
> of frogs, and our eyes with the molten sky. Feeling the
> polyrhythmic pulse of this place—this huge windswept
> body of water and stone. The vexed being in whose flesh
> we're entangled. Becoming earth. Becoming animal.
> Becoming, in this manner, fully human.   **DAVID ABRAM**

When guiding rewilding retreats and trainings, I often invite partici-
pants to take their hands out of their pockets and touch the land as
we walk, stalk, and crawl mindfully along. My good friend and fellow
mindful outdoor guide Mark Roule calls this practice "hiking with
hands." For many people, nature is no longer something to touch
and feel. Even sitting directly on the soft earth might feel strange and
scary. Yet the simple act of reaching out and feeling the different
types of tree bark can be a powerful awakening experience. Putting
your nose into the cracks of the bark can also be a surprise: white
pine furrows have a deep, earthy smell; cracking the twig of a sas-
safras tree releases a root beer–like aroma; popping a sap bubble on
a balsam has a piney scent like Christmas trees. The body's olfactory
system processes all the information in an odor, triggering reactions
and memories. Exploring the wide range of smells out on the land is
a wonderful way to draw closer to the earth.

Generally speaking, while exploring the outdoors, you needn't
worry about most plants. There are really only a few plants that you
want to avoid, and these are easy to identify. Poison ivy is common
around trails or disturbed areas, but it is sparse farther in the woods.
Poison ivy's shiny green leaves grow in threes on stems—hence, the
expression "Leaves of three, let it be"—and on hairy vines that go up
tree trunks or telephone poles. Poison oak is pretty rare and is found
in damp, sandy soil, usually at the edges of wetlands. Cow parsnip, or
wild parsnip, is a tall green plant with tiny yellow flowers that look a

little like Queen Anne's Lace. Its leaves grow symmetrically from the stem in groups of five, and the stem has deep grooves in it that you won't see in other plants. Of course, you also want to avoid any plants with obvious thorns or nettles. You can use your awakening sight to discern what to touch and what to steer clear of.

Our five primary senses (sight, hearing, touch, taste, and smell) evolved in relationship with our environment and other life-forms to become highly sensitive instruments that help us survive and thrive as a species. Perhaps you can recall walking behind someone wearing strong cologne or perfume. Now imagine that you can smell the musk of a buck or the odor of a bear that a spring breeze carries toward you. We still have the capacity; we need only to awaken our senses again. It's not enough simply to go outside. We also need to bring our attention and intention to the senses in order to consciously invoke, awaken, and sharpen their capabilities.

Our hunter-gatherer ancestors lived in simple shelters made of poles, straw mats, animal skins, and other natural objects. These human nests were often arranged in circles, following the way energy moves in nature, and they were permeable, allowing the sounds of the earth to filter in, along with drafts, which carried information. Although we've improved the functionality and comfort of our homes, we've also sealed ourselves off from the living, breathing world out there. As a result, many people who live mostly indoors suffer from sensory anesthesia, the gradual loss of sensory experience. Think about the number of plants growing in a forest or a field, the myriad decomposing life-forms washing around the ocean, the dry herbs and tree resins in a high desert plain. All these environments have their own concoction of smells, textures, sights, sounds, and flavors, richer and more varied than the average office environment.

In the woods and out on the land, the sense of smell is essential for survival. It can help us detect an incoming storm (think of the smell of the ozone before a thunderstorm) or the musk of a predator, like a skunk we want to avoid. To awaken this sense outdoors, I often invite folks to gather eastern hemlock or balsam needles, press them between their palms to release the aromatic oils, and then cup their hands and take deep inhalations. Another great stimulus for scent are the fallen leaves in autumn; crush them in your hands and take in their sweet, earthy smell.

During an outdoor mindfulness retreat I led with the Audubon Society one winter, we kept coming upon fox tracks in the snow. My cofacilitator, Dale, master naturalist and outdoor educator, kept sniffing and asking the group if we could smell the scent of fox on the air. At first the group was oblivious to it. Then Dale knelt down and lifted a small handful of snow with a small, yellow ice crystal in it, a drop of frozen fox urine. He invited us to take a whiff, and sure enough, it had a potent, musky, almost skunk-like smell. From then on, we were on our knees sniffing every little yellow patch of snow we found near fox tracks. After a few days, the group began picking up the smell on the wind.

You can feel a sensual connection with the living earth after only a few minutes of quiet and reflective nature meditation and observation. It may give you peace and joy, but it may also stir up other emotions, including grief—grief for species loss, environmental degradation, and climate change. Awakening our senses and countering sensory anesthesia is a practice of awareness, and when awareness expands, it perceives both pleasure and pain, light and dark, joy and sadness. That is why in the contemplative traditions there is an emphasis on clear seeing and calm abiding. We might be able to see the truth, to observe what is really happening, but can we handle it? Can we hold an experience of deep, clear perception without being totally swept away by it? We need to learn how to be with the expanding boundaries of our awareness. This comes as we develop a strong witness consciousness, that part of us that soars like an eagle and can see the big picture. When we can temper our increasing ability to feel with wisdom, we build our capacity of true spiritual growth.

Fascination Attention

What is life? It is the flash of a firefly in the night. It is the breath of a buffalo in the wintertime. It is the little shadow which runs across the grass and loses itself in the sunset. CROWFOOT, *Orator of the Blackfoot Confederacy*

I love to watch the wind blow through the trees or tall grass in a field, its invisible and mysterious qualities revealed through this interaction with the earth. The dance of light and shadows of clouds driven by the wind move across the body of the mountain behind my house. Sitting by a stream or near a beach, I'm mesmerized by the rhythm of the currents or waves. Such simple enjoyment of the beauty and wonder of nature is sometimes called "fascination attention." It is the opposite of "directed attention," which we employ when we are actively trying to hold our focus on a specific task or object, like when using the computer, attending meetings, or planning and strategizing. Directed attention is fatiguing, which is why when I get home from work, the perfect medicine for my tired brain is to stare at the mountain.

Nature is never truly still, and yet, the more still we become, the more we become aware of the subtle movements at play on the land. This vibration of life, the way the subtlest motion of air causes a single blade of grass to oscillate in the cool morning air, I refer to as *spanda*. In tantric yoga, *spanda* means "sacred tremor," which is present in all things. Spanda is the inflow and outflow of the breath, the movement of electrons, the turning of the earth on its axis and its orbit around the sun. Even things that may seem inert, like the "stone people" who sit so solidly in the earth, have spanda, their atoms vibrating below the level of our sensory awareness. The living earth embodies this sacred tremor, from the movement of our digestive tract to the movement of plate tectonics. We evolved enmeshed in the dance of spanda, carried by the movement of the seasons, the plants and animals, and the tides. It is in our nature to be drawn to the way things move and to be restored, nourished, and soothed by exposure to the land.

Focus allows us to get large and important projects done, but we can't sustain focus indefinitely. In meditation practice, there are two very similar types of meditative attention. One is often referred to as open awareness, where attention is not focused on a single thing but on the whole field of sensory input coming in at any given moment. Attention in this state is allowed to wander in the present moment, though not into the future or the past. The other type of attention is closed attention. An example of closed attention would be staring at the tip of your nose, focusing on a candle flame, or attending to the inflow and outflow of breath.

Environmental psychologists Rachel and Stephen Kaplan at the University of Michigan have done considerable research on the way natural environments can help to restore our ability to focus and support general resilience. Their terms, "directed attention" and "fascination attention," correspond nicely with the open and closed forms of meditative attention. Directed attention can be taxing over time because we have to block out or inhibit competing stimuli in order to hold our focus on a single object or task. This action of ongoing inhibition takes a toll and leads to what the Kaplans call "directed attention fatigue."[6] If the average American is looking at a screen for eleven hours a day, and almost entirely indoors, when they look up to take a break, it's likely they look up at an interior wall or some other human-made space. Contrast this with someone in an outdoor line of work who is focusing on a task, such as mowing or fixing a piece of equipment. After a period of directed attention, they can lift their gaze to see open land, trees, sky, or geese flying overhead.

To quote Yoshifumi Miyazaki, Japan's foremost researcher on forest bathing, "Throughout our evolution, we've spent 99.9 percent of our time in nature. Our physiology is still adapted to it. During everyday life, a feeling of comfort can be achieved if our rhythms are synchronized with those of the environment."[7]

Forest bathing contains elements of human rewilding, including deepening connection with the earth, awakening the senses, and learning to relate to trees and other nonhuman entities in the interconnected web of life. Originally, forest bathing was developed to help stressed urbanites in Japan cope with the challenges of city living and demanding careers. Today it has spread all over the world and has opened a new (and old) doorway for modern humans to come home to the many gifts and opportunities in their local forests. Forest bathing invites us into a deeper relationship with trees, particularly evergreens with their fresh, bright, and invigorating aromas.

Forest Bathing and Other Invitations

> It is not so much for its beauty that the forest
> makes a claim upon men's hearts, as for that subtle
> something, that quality of air, that emanation from
> old trees, that so wonderfully changes and renews a
> weary spirit.   ROBERT LOUIS STEVENSON

My family and I live close to Mount Greylock, at 3,489 feet the high-est mountain in Massachusetts. Part of the Appalachians, the oldest mountain chain in North America, Mount Greylock also contains one of the southernmost boreal forests on the continent. This alpine eco-system evolved to survive the extreme winter weather of the region, which is particularly brutal on the exposed mountain peaks, home to a forest of balsam firs, which are cold tolerant—remarkably, their boughs can flex to accommodate heavy loads of winter snow.

In the warmer months, Greylock is perfect for walking, particularly because the balsams give off loads of essential oils, also known as phy-toncides. These aromatics boost immunity and elevate mood, and in fact, everyone on the Greylock trail is wonderfully friendly. It's a stark contrast from the experience of walking through a chain store, where smiles and eye contact are rare. Hiking up Greylock is a sacred tradi-tion for my family. When we are on the mountain, my kids seldom argue or fuss. They, too, seem to be elevated by the energy of the place. Walking up the Appalachian Trail in the damp coolness of the balsams' shade, I feel my worries and tensions transform and melt, like frost in the morning sun. Above the din of traffic and human commerce, the air moves differently, and I feel above it all, like I am on a higher plane of reality.

Throughout this forest, the wonderful smell of pine fills the atmo-sphere, freshens the senses, and stimulates the mind. I do a lot of mindful breathing and tend to pause often to take deep breaths, which has a calming effect on the mind and body. This practice is enhanced on Greylock by the concentration of essential oils in the air. In ancient times, pine boughs were believed to ward off evil spirits and disease. Today, research into the power of phytoncides bears out this ancient belief in pine's medicinal attributes. Essential oil, tea made from the needles, and ointment made from the pine resin have all been shown to have healing properties.

Up on Greylock, the balsams' intoxicating aroma and the misty air combine to create a kind of tonic, as if the mountain's exhalations were a potent medicine and we are absorbed in its breath. I really can't overstate the power of these balsams. They are literally a forest of feral Christmas trees. Pre-Christian cultures saw evergreen trees as symbols of renewal, and some brought cuttings inside during winter, when the sun is at its weakest. I also love the tradition of bringing a fresh balsam inside our home for the Christmas season. These trees have long reminded us that days will grow long again and that earth's green life will return, even after the longest and coldest winters. Marking the solstices and equinoxes today with rituals rooted in nature, as our ancestors did, can help orient us in time, season, and place.

I've been mindfully engaging with woods like this for decades, but since learning about the practice of forest bathing, I am grateful to have this clear term to explain how I intuitively relate to the woods. When forest bathing, you mindfully commune with the forest environment to relieve stress and anxiety, elevate your mood, boost your immunity, bond with nature, and find inspiration in its beauty. Forest bathing is less about getting to a destination and more about experiencing wherever you happen to be, so it is accessible to more people.

Forest bathing in Japanese is *shinrin yoku*, a term coined by Tomohide Akiyama, a director of the Japanese Forestry Agency. *Shinrin* means "forest," and *yoku* means "to bathe." The official definition of the practice is "taking in, in all of our senses, the forest atmosphere."[8]

Shinrin yoku is not about roughing it in the wilderness; forest-bathing stations in Japan have bathrooms and concession stands. And no, it does not involve taking a shower in the woods. The idea is to make the forest accessible so that you can receive the therapeutic benefits of immersing all five senses in the forest's embrace.

In 1990, Dr. Yoshifumi Miyazaki of Chiba University measured the effects of shinrin yoku and found these proven benefits:

- reduces physiological stress, depressive symptoms, and hostility

- improves sleep, vigor, and feelings of aliveness

- lowers cortisol levels

- lowers blood pressure and pulse rate

- increases heart rate variability

- decreases blood flow to the prefrontal cortex

- improves immune system functioning due to decrease in stress hormones[9]

Forest bathing's benefits go far beyond stress reduction and immune boosting. It also fosters a connection between human beings and nature, which contributes to human rewilding. Over the past thirty years, Dr. Miyazaki and others have gathered scientific evidence for the health benefits of forest bathing. They have also partnered with the healthcare industry to make forest bathing part of a holistic approach to well-being. Because of Miyazaki's research, we can say that walking mindfully in a forest is forest bathing, though communing with nature is not a practice that belongs to any one culture or people. People from every corner of the globe have long remarked on the health-giving properties of nature.

The World Health Organization found that in 2008, for the first time in history, the majority of people live in urban environments, making us now a predominantly urban species.[10] WHO has also found that noncommunicable diseases, or lifestyle diseases, now account for more than half of the premature deaths in the developed world.[11] These diseases are the direct result of the stress, poor diet, and lack of exercise that are the way we now live in modern society. People need intimate contact with nature. We need to bathe in its beauty, eat its simple foods, and stay on the move. Forest bathing and other practices for connecting with nature improve our physical and mental health. We also need to observe and learn from nature's cycles to be inspired by her wisdom. We need to honor the turning of the seasons and feel ourselves living within the great wheel of life.

The power of life that is experienced so directly through nature has gone by many names. In yoga that life power is referred to as *prana*; in Taoism, the *tao*; in Chinese medicine, *chi*; in Shinto, *kami*; in Lakota, *Wakan Tanka*; and in the modern mythology of *Star Wars*, the *force*. This ancient concept that nature is interconnected and imbued with consciousness is no longer confined to mythology and religion. The modern science of quantum mechanics has uncovered evidence of the interbeing that Thich Nhat Hanh and many contemplative traditions hold central. When we peer deeply into nature, we see that every entity exists in relation to everything else.

Human health and planetary health are inextricably combined. In my own communing with nature, it isn't about using the forest for my own well-being but about realizing that my well-being and the well-being of the forest are the same, that together we are nature experiencing itself through a highly developed nervous system, capable of great depth of feeling and self-reflection. Forest bathing is a way to awaken our own consciousness within the supportive matrix of the forest's wisdom.

GUIDED FOREST BATHING

Before embarking on a walk in a forest or a park with trees, take a few moments to bring your full attention into the present moment. Invite a deep breath in and a long, slow breath out. Do this three to five times. Feel your feet on the ground and the sky opening above you. Imagine that your body, like the trunk of a tree, is rooted and grounded in the earth while also connected to the infinite sky above. Feel your body as a channel of awareness connecting heaven and earth. Breathing into the space inside your body and exhaling into the space all around you, sense the embodied experience of being both alone and intimately connected to the forest that surrounds you.

Notice the sounds of the forest. What can you hear?

Notice the sensation of the air on your skin. How does it feel? Is it hot? Cold? Warm? Cool?

Notice what you can smell. What does the air smell like? What does this tell you about your surroundings?

When you are ready, open your eyes and look around. Without naming anything, just notice the colors, shapes, textures, and depth of field. What do you see?

When you are ready, begin walking with an awareness of each step. Walk as if you are blessing the earth with each step. Take in the forest atmosphere through all of your senses. As you walk, feel free to reach out and gently caress the bark of trees or the moss on stones, or place your hands in cool running water and feel the current or the mud or the stones in the stream. Allow your body to come into sensual contact with the land.

If you notice something beautiful or interesting, allow yourself to pause and explore. You have no destination. You are already here. Allow yourself to experience being in this forest. Keep coming back to your breath.

If you'd like, find a nice spot to sit and relax. Give yourself a few minutes to just rest here and observe the forest. Allow yourself to be still and to notice any and all movement around you, however small.

When you feel complete, walk mindfully back to where you started. Pause again and take a deep breath in, letting it go with a sigh and with a sign of thanks to the forest.

Impermanence: Wisdom of Blossoms and Falling Leaves

The natural world freely gives lessons in rewilding. One timeless lesson is that of impermanence. Any mindful work in nature is bound to elicit awareness of life's constant changes and to stir feelings associated with loss and new beginnings. The impermanence of life is on constant display in nature. Siddhartha Gautama, the Buddha, realized that human suffering was caused by attachment to pleasure and aversion to pain and discomfort. His prescription to end suffering is the practice of nonattachment. Because everything in life is impermanent and only change is constant, we practice letting go of our attachments and embrace impermanence.

This is a difficult practice.

> You must train yourself to let go of that
> which you fear to lose the most.   YODA

A perfect example of the celebration of impermanence in Japanese culture is *Hanami*, the Cherry Blossom Festival, which occurs each spring. Cherry and plum blossoms bloom in aromatic pink petals and sometimes last only a day. As in New England during the peak of the colors of autumn, people in Japan flock to see and smell the stunning aromatic blossoms, enjoying the beauty of that short season, a lesson in the beauty of impermanence.

Nature is always teaching us about change. By embracing impermanence as part of our forest bathing and rewilding practice, we can begin to experience so much more of what nature has to share, whether it be the lush fullness of summer or the depths of the bleak midwinter.

I have two favorite *Hanami*-like seasons here in western Massachusetts. The first happens in May, when the crabapple tree in our backyard is in full bloom. On a good year, the entire tree, which is about twenty feet high and has a wide crown, blooms into a giant pink marshmallow. When a soft breeze blows, delicate pink petals flutter to the young spring grass, creating a surreal pink carpet that gives off a light floral bouquet. The flowers last only a couple of days, which makes the whole experience that much more potent and special. My kids and

I spend as much time as we can just lying in the grass and the petals, looking up at the mountain and breathing it in. If the cherry blossoms blooming in Japan exceed the glory of a blooming crabapple in May, they must be glorious indeed.

My other favorite season of impermanence is in October, when the leaves begin to change. A dyed-in-the-wool New Englander, I love our mixed hardwood forests, our seasons, and our old stone fences. When fall rolls around, I could lie in the leaves for days and watch the mountains change color.

Autumn is a celebration of impermanence. First, the sugar maples turn, sometime in early September. They go out in a blaze of glory, all bright oranges and scarlets. The oaks, hickories, and poplars turn next. They go from green to yellow and brown, from soft and juicy to tough and leathery. Then they start dropping their acorns and hickory nuts, which the squirrels and chipmunks gather up as quickly as they hit the ground. Next, the beeches turn, like a grand finale in a fireworks display. Mother Nature saves the best for last. The beeches' smooth grey trunks look like elephant legs in the forest, and their simple toothed leaves resemble elegant elven boats, as they float down clear woodland streams, rolling over miniature waterfalls, and swirling in the eddies of little pools. The leaves go from green to brown and then to silvery golden, sometimes at the same time on the same leaf, and they hang on to their branches and quiver in the cold autumn winds. Beech leaves quaking in a breeze are one of the most beautiful things to be seen in the forests of the world. They are stalwart and stubborn, perhaps afraid of what happens after they let go and give themselves to the wind. Are we any different?

I have a favorite patch of forest near Lake Mahkeenac in Stockbridge, Massachusetts, where I like to guide my groups. The trail winds through a forest of mixed hardwoods and evergreens, passing several massive eastern white pine trees, one of which is home to an impressive nest for a bird of prey we have not yet identified. As the trail nears the edge of the lake, a wetland separates the forest environment from the open water. This edge, or ecotone, is rich with wildlife activity. It also has a white pine that is so big it takes four people to wrap their arms around its trunk. This tree is also noteworthy because it pitches at about a 55-degree tilt toward the lake. This makes it perfect for sitting against, with your bottom cushioned by an ancient carpet of pine needles.

I once walked in these woods on a bitter cold November Sunday with my son, Stryder, when he was four, and my good friend and mentor Moose, the groundskeeper and land steward at Kripalu. On that particular morning, Stryder sat down at the base of this tree, closed his eyes, and interlaced his little fingers in a prayer mudra. He sat there, and from what I could tell, prayed or meditated for a full five minutes. I observed him in wonder as my heart filled up to the brim and spilled over with love and gratitude for such a perfect moment.

I recently led another group to this same location, about four years after Stryder and I visited. On our way to the leaning tree, we found three clusters of barred-owl feathers. It seemed an owl had been eaten by some other bird of prey, perhaps another barred owl (known to hunt their own kind to protect their territory) or a great horned owl. I carried one of the feathers with me as we walked through the forest, attuning myself to the creature for whom this feather had enabled flight and vision from high perspectives. As we made our way toward the leaning pine, someone in our group spotted a barred owl high up in a hemlock tree. We paused for ten minutes to observe this large, noble creature, apparently napping about forty feet up, occasionally opening one eye to check on us. I felt compelled to silently thank this owl for the gift of its presence. I took the feather I was carrying, which was perhaps a victim of this mighty owl's skills in hunting and territorial protection, and placed it in the bark of a hemlock beside me. We then made our way to the great leaning pine.

Moose let me know that the big tree had recently broken off, about ten feet up, and fallen to the ground. In my heart, I felt the loss of this mighty tree, and as we drew close to it, we could smell the scent of pine on the air from the exposed inner wood. I placed my hands on the trunk and thought of all this tree had lived through and of that morning when my son sat protected at its base.

I invited the group to spread out and find a place to sit for a nature meditation. As we settled into our spots, we heard the cawing of numerous crows coming close and then dive-bombing the barred owl in its perch. The wind kicked up and blew cold and hard through the trees. In the distance we heard screams. A fox? Kids playing? It was hard to tell. Nevertheless, the sound was unsettling. As we continued to sit, I couldn't help but feel sadness at the demise of the great tree, also a reminder of my son's childhood passing by so quickly. I felt my heart opening big, vulnerable to the sweetness of life's temporary treasures. Life's impermanence was on display so fully on this morning in the winter woods. As we gathered together in a circle to share our experiences, one woman said that the fallen tree had brought the memory of her recently deceased brother into her awareness. Tears flowed down her cheeks as she shared memories of their childhood, though she appreciated the opportunity to feel the loss and the gift of her brother's life.

A fallen tree can awaken such depth of feeling. Our species evolved, after all, in deep connection with trees. Perhaps the natural world, in its many manifestations and life-forms, reflects back to us our own inner environment. While in mindful relationship with the earth, we try to stay with the feelings that arise. Impermanence is all around us, and though we may try to build walls of security, nature eventually washes them away or blows them down. It is in surrendering and opening to this essential impermanence of nature that we can begin to live in harmony with our world, taking each moment as a gift and giving thanks for the moments we have, as precious and miraculous as they are.

Kami, the Spirit of Place

I spend a lot of time walking off trails and exploring the various nooks and crannies of the lands here in western Massachusetts. I love to feel the tug of the land calling me off the well-trodden path and into some hollow or glen around the bend or over the hill. I find that the more I get to know a place, the more the land speaks to me and in some cases guides me to new special places. Each place has a story, a history, and a character. Rewilding invites us to become students of the land, to open ourselves up to the wisdom that geography has to share.

When Buddhism arrived in Japan, the kingdom was home to a pantheistic religion known as Shinto, which regards all of nature as infused with the quality referred to as *kami*. *Kami* can mean "sacred essence" and is believed to emanate from natural beings such as rocks, rivers, and trees, as well as animals, including people. Shintoism is animistic, like many indigenous cultures the world over, and views nature as imbued by many spirits, gods, and goddesses. The land and elements are considered very much alive, and Shinto rituals and ceremonies seek to honor and align with these forces.

As a child I walked in the New England woods with my mother, who loves collecting rocks and studying Native American cultures. Through her example and guidance, I developed a sensitivity to the character of the land, to the rocks and to the trees. I pay attention to the landscape to read its expressions and to feel its moods. The more time you spend on the land, really exploring and becoming intimate with its character and qualities, the more you will get a feel for what kami is about.

You may find yourself drawn to a place based on an intuition. Places have their own energy and memory. Stones and old trees have been around a lot longer than we have, and stones will be here long after we have gone. The more of our attention we give to a place, the stronger the bond we will feel. Our senses become sharper, and we see more clearly where we are. We develop the eyes to see and the ears to hear the voice and spirit of the land.

The mountain behind my house is bordered by a thickly vegetated floodplain. In the summer, the area is practically impassable, with ferns that grow chest high and green briar that forms a natural fence. Living at the foot of this mountain, I have ventured into this area in all seasons, gradually learning ways to get through at different times of the year. The density of the vegetation provides a sanctuary for wildlife of all kinds. On snowy and muddy days, I have tracked black bears, bobcats, coyotes, foxes, fisher cats, skunks, raccoons, squirrels, otters, mice, turkey, crows, an occasional human, and a variety of smaller birds.

As the years go by, I get to know my marsh and my mountain more and more. I know some individual trees very well. We have one tree that we call "Coyote Bridge" because it lies across our brook, and the first time we found it, a coyote had pooped on it. Now it's our bridge, and my children are learning about balance and footing as they cross it in all seasons and weather. I am bonded to this land. I have come to love it deeply. The fact that my children are growing up playing barefoot on its breast deepens the bond even more.

Wabi, Appreciating Transient Beauty

Rewilding is an ethic that elevates the simple, the handmade, and the practical. Unlike the consumer obsession with all that is shiny and new, the journey of rewilding guides us into relationship with that which is old and worn. Along with the Shinto idea of kami, Japanese philosophy has a unique appreciation for things that are naturally worn, battered, and otherwise shaped by time and natural forces. I have found this concept to be helpful in appreciating the rough beauty of nature in its raw and wild forms. Think of a boulder covered in moss, a rusty old tractor in a snowy expanse, or the sun-bleached bones of an animal lying on a windswept field. This is *wabi*.

This aesthetic was one of the ingredients that set the *Star Wars* films apart from other science fiction films of its era. Unlike the *Buck Rogers* and *Star Trek* franchises, which displayed clean and shiny spaceships and explorers in crisp, clean uniforms, *Star Wars* made space look old, beat-up, and rugged, like a spaghetti western or an old Kurosawa flick. We love the Millennium Falcon because it's dented and worn. It has scars and stories. That is also what wabi is all about.

Often when I am forest bathing, wandering, or rambling through the woods, I notice something old and worn that is so achingly beautiful I have to stop and just be with it. Recently, I was exploring a cobble on the ridge near where I live. A cobble is an open, rocky spot where you are likely to find mosses, lichen, and smaller, stunted trees. On this particular spot, you will find all of that plus lots of lowbush blueberry and wintergreen growing all around. As I was sauntering along, I saw an old maple log that had fallen over years ago. It was hollow and lying on its side so that it formed a long bowl, with the opening gazing up to the sky. In the bowl, a thick carpet of mosses and lichens had grown. A dash of red and orange maple leaves added flair. It was the most stunning little piece of terrarium gardening, and it was just out there, as natural as could be. I could have sat with that old log for hours, just looking around, as the cool autumn wind blew the leaves down into that cobble.

Wabi fills a void in our western vernacular. We don't have a word like wabi that combines the qualities of rugged, worn, and beautiful. Wabi can promote a greater appreciation for used things, and perhaps encourage more repairing and less disposing. It can also help us see the earth through a different lens. If we can begin to embrace what is old and worn in nature as beautiful, it is more likely we will bring that appreciation back home.

The living earth, of which we are a thinking, feeling, breathing and self-reflective expression, is both within us and around us. We find our greatest solace and sense of place when we mindfully dwell in the awareness of our inherent state of connection with all that is. Spending mindful time outdoors, observing, feeling, and interacting with our local environment can help us build embodied experiences of this calm, clear, and connected state of being. It is not enough to think about such lofty ideas; we have to get out there and engage with the land, the more-than-human world, and our fellow humans. As a father, I am committed to doing what I can to ensure that we live an earth-centered, sustainable life, for the benefit of the planet and future generations. We need to be strong for the times we are living in. Turning toward the wisdom of the earth will help us find our footing and give us the physical, mental, and spiritual healing we need. Mindful rewilding can help us be the change our time is calling for. No matter how long it has been, a feeling of being connected, supported, and at home on earth is just a few breaths and a few steps outside.

SKILLS ARE THE DOORWAY TO AWARENESS,
AND AWARENESS IS THE DOORWAY TO SPIRIT.

STALKING WOLF

4

RECLAIMING SKILLS

Movement, Preparedness, Fire, and Shelter

The average modern human has no idea how to walk in the woods. Shoes turn most people's feet into iron-clad tanks that crash and crush, so that they have no awareness of what is underfoot. The modern shoe is the house of the foot, creating a tight seal that separates our feeling and sensing feet from the textures and contours of the living earth. Perhaps it was reading about Hobbits that first inspired me to want to walk through the woods quietly and with awareness. According to Tolkien, Hobbits are known for this ability. As a kid, I used to practice jumping from rock to rock on the trails in the woods around my father's house. I noticed early on that stepping lightly on stones made my footsteps almost completely silent, while stepping on dry leaves, twigs, and branches made lots of noise. As boys, we'd spend days upon days playing soldier or Kick the Can, and the need to sneak made learning to move quietly a valuable skill.

Of course, as I grew up and began to learn to meditate, I became more sensitive to the mood of the lands I was exploring and the way that my own movement and presence disturbed what Tom Brown Jr. calls "the baseline" of the forest, or the sounds and activity that occur when there is no disturbance or sense of threat among the creatures of the forest. The birds, squirrels, and other creatures are going about their day, when suddenly three hikers enter the forest, stepping on twigs, talking loudly, and setting off multiple "alarms" as every forest resident calls out a warning. In a few moments, the forest is silent, and everyone has fled or is staying out of sight until the intruders are gone. Each time we move on the land, we create what Tom Brown Jr. calls "concentric rings," like those of a pebble tossed into a pond. It takes awareness and skill to move over land without creating big rings of disturbance. When we arrive in our nature location to meditate, it takes ten to fifteen minutes before our concentric rings die down and the forest baseline returns to normal.

While sitting quietly in the woods, I have often been startled to see a deer appear only yards away, as if the deer had been teleported to that location without making the slightest sound. Deer are masters at moving silently through the terrain and blending in with their environment. In fact, their primary defense is stealth. When deer walk, they place each hoof with precision.

For most of us, not knowing how to walk with awareness isn't really our fault. We were never taught how to breathe properly or to move with awareness and skill through the woods.

Walking with Awareness

Here is an awareness practice for walking in the woods, which I call "Don't Step on a Twig!" The goal with this walking meditation is to avoid stepping on twigs and making loud sounds that startle the forest. In order not to do this, though, there are a few things you need to do.

The first is that you need to pay attention to how you are walking. Most of us walk heel to toe, which means that when we take a step, our heel lands first and then we roll onto the front of the foot. This way of walking came about when we started wearing shoes with heels for walking in cities and on cobblestone streets. On hard surfaces, there is less need to be gentle and skillful with our gait. When our ancestors walked barefoot, however, they walked toe to heel. They explored the terrain with the ball of the big toe, rolled their weight out to the pinky toe side of the foot, and then gradually lowered the heel. When you walk this way, you have much more awareness of the terrain and can avoid applying too much downward pressure on twigs and sticks, which will prevent you from making a lot of noise.

Try to walk this way barefoot at home before trying it in a park or in the woods and notice the difference: Lift your foot slowly, place the ball of the big toe first, feeling to make sure that the surface below doesn't make a sound. Then roll to the outer edge of your foot, still sensing the surface below, and adjusting accordingly. Slowly and mindfully, lower your heel down. If you sense something under your heel, do not lower it all the way down. Instead, keep the weight on the front of your foot as you lift the other foot to continue walking. You'll need to keep your knees slightly bent, and you may even place your hands on your thighs just above your knees for support. Tom Brown Jr. and Jon Young call this "the Fox Walk."

You will also need to walk more slowly and mindfully than you normally do. If you do this while breathing consciously, the combination of breath awareness and slow, mindful steps will completely change your experience when you're outdoors moving over land and through different ecosystems. You may also begin to relate more deeply to deer medicine and find yourself blending into the landscape.

It is important to pause regularly when walking in this way and to pay attention to what is moving all around you. Over time you will find that your senses get stronger.

The Wisdom of Wood

As a child, I lived in a home that was made almost entirely of wood, with exposed beams, one of which was salvaged from an old farm house. It must have been at least 150 years old. In bed, I would stare up at beams made of cedar. There was always something comforting about those beams; their grain and texture provided something to ponder. As I tried to fall asleep, I might also stare down at the wood-plank floor. The knots and grain of each plank morphed into faces or scenes in my mind. The pattern of wood is one we have known forever, and there is much to see when meditating on its qualities.

Wood is our friend. Trees give us much of the air we breathe, shade us from the hot sun, feed us with their fruits and nuts, and extend branches we can climb to get higher and see farther than normal. They also give of their bodies so that we may eat and so that we may fashion tools and other objects that allow us to thrive on this good earth. Trees are alive, and their wood is a gift. When walking among them, be respectful. Never harm a tree unnecessarily, for they do feel and sense their world. When gathering wood for a fire or harvesting a live tree to fashion a tool, please use it wisely and with reverence.

Invite an ethic of reciprocity and gratitude into your rewilding. It affirms the reality that everything is connected and that when we take, we have a responsibility to give back, so that the equilibrium of living communities stays in balance. Often this is a personal and even private affair, a prayer of thankfulness upon finding wintergreen berries in the snow or offering a pine cone mandala in gratitude for a beautiful sunset. These gestures may at first feel childlike, even silly, but they open powerful doorways in our awareness and open our hearts to the universe.

Prayer is speaking to that which you consider to be divine, transcendent, holy. To pray in nature is to speak to and with the Great Mystery. In my own experience, praying outdoors allows the more-than-human world to interact with me in moments of vulnerable conversation with the mystery of life. Whatever your outlook or belief system, allowing yourself time and space to practice speaking from your heart, directly to the source of life, is restorative and positive.

Outside the enclosed walls of human-made spaces, the holy air moves and speaks; birds punctuate our thoughts with songs, calls, or alarms; birds of prey soar overhead, and clouds cover or reveal the life-giving light of our home star. When the spirits of the land move in times of heartfelt and reverent conversation with God, connections are nourished between us and all living things. We may find ourselves embraced physically, emotionally, and spiritually in a much larger family than we usually find ourselves in. Feelings of loneliness and isolation give way to wonder, awe, and profound gratitude for the gift of life and the beauty of this living earth.

At one time, a vast array of skills ensured our ancestors' survival as they lived in intimate reciprocity with their environment. Knowing the plant beings and animals with whom we share our land, reading the weather, being able to birth fire, fashion shelter, and make the tools and other necessary items for living day to day are essential aspects of human rewilding. I have found great joy in learning and mastering these skills. Whether it is bringing forth fire in the palm of your hand, making nutritious tea from the abundant needles of coniferous trees in your region, or knowing how to create a shelter that will keep you alive in adverse conditions, these utilitarian skills are also spiritually nourishing. And they address our innate need for connection with the living earth.

Mindful awareness helps us to experience survival skills, as they are sometimes called, in an entirely different light. We're not working from a frontier mentality that considers nature something savage and brutal we humans are meant to tame and conquer. We also don't consider nature a two-dimensional warehouse of resources meant for our exploitation. Using these ancient skills can help us to come into right relationship with the earth and ourselves. They can open doorways of awareness that deepen our connection with the sacred web of life, in which we are nested, helping us to rediscover our place in the universe.

I discovered this to be true in my own journey of integrating mindfulness with ancestral skills. Most meditative traditions have deep roots in nature and remote wilderness. The forests, mountains, deserts, and jungles of the world have long called out to those seeking the answers to life's deepest questions. Why then shouldn't these worlds be bridged again by the basic skills of living in intimate relationship with nature, so that those who feel drawn to the great mysteries of life can also feel more confident, more empowered, and more self-sustained? Rewilding can connect us with the real world, our first world. Knowing that I can fashion a shelter if I need to, or make a fire and otherwise see to my basic survival needs gives me a sense of assuredness, relaxation, and calm.

Recently I was hiking up a mountain with my children, who are now six and eight. My littlest one, Cora, said to me, "Daddy, if the sun went down and we were stuck up on this mountain, you could scrape your knife on your fire stick and make fire for us and build a debris hut. We'd be okay, wouldn't we, Daddy?"

"Yes, Cora, we'd be okay," I said with a reassuring wink.

We've spent enough time outdoors, making fires, foraging, and building shelters that she feels safe far from the comforts of home, and as her dad, knowing that she is comfortable and confident warms my heart. For at the end of the day, what is my primary function in this life if not to help my children feel safe, self-assured, and positive in the world they inhabit? Feeling safe begins with feeling comfortable with the planet itself, with different environments, the weather, and other living creatures. This familiarity sets the stage for a sense of belonging and a positive outlook on life. With a strong bond to a place, knowledge of the local flora and fauna, and a core set of skills for attending to your basic needs outdoors, you will enjoy a fulfilling, lifelong relationship with a greater power.

I believe that everyone benefits from knowing how to attend to their own basic survival needs. The ability to find or create shelter, birth fire, treat water, fashion necessary tools, and forage or hunt for food will make anyone feel more secure away from modern industrial society. These abilities also place you in direct communication with the living earth, where the greatest gifts can be found. Having these skills will not only save your life if you are ever in the wild on your own, they also have the power to save your soul from a nature-deprived life. Learning to make a fire, becoming familiar with wild

Dear Sounds True friend,

Since 1985, Sounds True has been sharing spiritual wisdom and resources to help people live more genuine, loving, and fulfilling lives. We hope that our programs inspire and uplift you, enabling you to bring forth your unique voice and talents for the benefit of us all.

We would like to invite you to become part of our growing online community by giving you three downloadable programs—an introduction to the treasure of authors and artists available at Sounds True! To receive these gifts, just flip this card over for details, then visit us at **SoundsTrue.com/Free** and enter your email for instant access.

With love on the journey,

TAMI SIMON   Founder and Publisher, Sounds True

sounds true
many voices, one journey   800.333.9185

Free Audio Programs!

The Self-Acceptance Project ($97 value)
Instant access to 23 respected spiritual teachers and more than 26 hours of transformational teachings on self-compassion, especially during challenging times.

The Practice of Mindfulness ($15 value)
Download guided practices by Jon Kabat-Zinn, Shinzen Young, Kelly McGonigal, Tara Brach, Sharon Salzberg, and Jack Kornfield.

Meditation Music ($10 value)
Listen to nine inspiring tracks for healing, relaxation, and releasing stress.

To download these **3 free gifts** go to **SoundsTrue.com/Free**

800.333.9185

SOUNDS TRUE
many voices, one journey

edibles in your area, being able to improvise a shelter, staying warm, and seeing the silver moon through the tree branches are all a kind of vital medicine. These skills give us access to a vital part of our inner nature and place us in direct contact with the earth and the universe in a grounded and embodied way.

Years ago, when I first learned the skill of making fire through the bow-drill method (which we will explore later in this chapter), I proposed leading a workshop on it at a retreat center. I told the retreat programmer that people need to know this skill. She seemed perplexed and said, "Micah, that is a very cool thing, but why does anyone need to know how to do this?" At the time, I was so surprised by her reaction that I was not sure how to respond. It seemed obvious to me that this was a vital skill. The experience of spinning the spindle into the hearthboard until aromatic cedar smoke begins to billow and a tiny glowing coal comes alive is one of the most profound things I had ever experienced. But the programmer did not know the power of that experience, and from a purely utilitarian perspective, she had a point—after all, we have lighters and matches now. Why would anyone need to know how to do this anymore?

So many things have been made easy for us. We don't need to walk as much because we have cars, mass transit, electric skateboards, and Segways to move our bodies around the world. Our food is packaged, seasoned, and ready to eat. With the consolidation and mechanization of agriculture, there are fewer and fewer farms, and with the robot revolution currently under way, millions of manufacturing jobs will disappear over the next couple of decades. There are even automated electric lawn mowers for those who do not want to deal with maintaining one of the last vestiges of "nature" in the suburbs. What is there left for us to do? Many of the giant tech companies are talking about basic universal income for the masses, yet even if that happens, what are we to do with ourselves? Is this good for us? I can remember when the video game *Rock Band* was all the rage. I wondered if a whole generation of kids would grow up learning to play air guitar and never know the joy that comes from actually working hard over time to play a real guitar and actually rock.

A lot of kids grow up without learning to split wood or to whittle, to ride horses or motorbikes, to fish or to climb trees. Some people are going decades without allowing their bare feet to touch the ground. We have created technological worlds, and we are learning to navigate the internet and write code, pretending that this human-made world is apart from the support and grace of the natural world outside. I believe it is essential for our well-being as a species and for the well-being of the planet and the other species we share it with to stay connected to the old ways, to our hunting and gathering heritage.

> Humanity today is like a waking dreamer, caught
> between the fantasies of sleep and the chaos of the real
> world. The mind seeks but cannot find the precise place
> and hour. We have created a Star Wars civilization, with
> Stone Age emotions, medieval institutions, and godlike
> technology. We thrash about. We are terribly confused
> by the mere fact of our existence, and a danger to
> ourselves and to the rest of life.   E. O. WILSON[1]

I am not advocating a Luddite approach, where we have to throw our iPhones in the trash and live off the grid, although there is nothing wrong with choosing to go that way. I am suggesting that most people would benefit from regularly logging off the internet and logging on to the "wood-wide-web." The average person has a need now and then for a crackling fire, wind in their hair, a refreshing swim, the weight and balance of a stout walking stick, and the feeling of being sheltered by the flesh and bones of the land. Our biology has not changed since we moved indoors. Our love for open spaces, water, high ground, and trees is baked into our physiology. Our need for refuge and for a place from which we can look out with a higher and wider perspective is an integral part of who we are. We still need to know that we are an integral part of this earth, that we belong, and that whatever continent our ancestors came from, we can endeavor to become "naturalized" to the land on which we now live.

In the pages ahead, we're going to explore some basic skills for rewilding your life. This chapter is by no means a comprehensive guide. Think of it more as a starting point to get you on your way. The knowledge and skills of our ancestors, on every continent, are vast and deep. I like to remind myself to stay humble no matter what because there is always more to learn. These words from Isaac Newton offer good inspiration:

> I do not know what I may appear to the world, but to myself I seem to have been only like a boy playing on the seashore, and diverting myself in now and then finding a smoother pebble or a prettier shell than ordinary, whilst the great ocean of truth lay all undiscovered before me.[2]

Being Prepared

An essential discipline for being outdoors is to get into the habit of being prepared. This means checking the weather ahead of time, dressing appropriately, and bringing along any additional layers and gear you may need for a changing forecast. Here are some important guidelines to keep in mind.

1. **Weather.** Check the weather and plan accordingly. Having a good weather app on your phone is important. If you can install weather updates, this can be helpful, too, especially having a function that will alert you to lightning strikes in your area. This first tip about using your phone may seem to go against my earlier advice about putting away your phone when in the wild. In my work we have two rules about phones in the field. Rule Number One: Use your phone to check the weather to stay safe and to call 911 in an emergency. Rule Number Two: Stow the phone. We put away the phone so that we can enjoy nature through our senses. That said, because weather can be

the determining factor that affects our safety outdoors, up-to-the-minute weather updates are invaluable.

2. **Stay found.** Always let someone know where you are going to be when heading into the field and also when you plan on getting back. I recommend getting to know a particular place near where you live, perhaps the same general area where you go for your nature meditation. Get to know this place well through all seasons. When you decide to explore a new, nearby territory, orient yourself to the topography of the place you know. Study maps of the terrain and notice other landmarks. Stay on the trail unless or until you are very familiar with a place. Get into the habit of finding your current location on a map so that, in the event of an emergency, you will be able to know where you are and chart a course home.

3. **Clothing.** "There is no such thing as bad weather, just bad clothing," according to a Norwegian proverb. Dress appropriately for the season and the terrain. If there's a possibility that you could get wet and that the temperature could drop, do not wear cotton clothing if possible. If you are exploring an area where you gain in elevation, know that weather can change quickly, especially in the summer. Wearing layers and having extra layers in a backpack is key to comfort in most outdoor settings. The tropics are an exception to carrying extra layers, but there, too, you want to have a breathable base layer. Elsewhere, your breathable base layer can be merino wool, which wicks moisture away from your body. Your mid-layers can be a fleece jacket or a wool sweater and a water-and-windproof outer layer, such as the Gore-Tex brand. The value of a good outer layer can't be overstated. It is like having a wearable tent. To complete your outdoor attire, a pair of waterproof pants, a hat, gloves, and extra socks (in case the ones you're wearing get wet)

are also essential. The goal is to stay dry. Hypothermia is the number one killer outdoors, so staying dry and warm is always your goal. With appropriate clothing you can be outside for days and maintain your core body temperature.

In the outdoor trainings I lead, we are outside in the shoulder seasons for nine-day intensives. Weather in western Massachusetts can vary wildly in the spring, early summer, and fall. We are out for twelve hours a day, in cold, driving rain, snow, mud, and temperatures ranging from the mid-20s to the upper 70s. When everyone comes prepared, we can be outside without worry for over a week and have a great time, so we emphasize the importance of proper clothing. It's about safety first and foremost, but it's also about feeling at home outdoors and staying in that home longer.

What to Bring?

Depending on your plans for the day, there are a lot of possible gear combinations you might like to bring with you to be prepared. Here are two levels of preparedness to guide your plan.

The Park Bag

If you are heading into a small park or other outdoor area where you won't ever be more than a few hundred yards or so from the human world, you don't really need to bring too much with you. Here are a few essentials: cell phone, a small first aid kit, water, snacks, emergency whistle, field guide, map, extra layer, hat. I recommend having a small hip or backpack preloaded and ready to go, so that when the mood strikes, you can grab and go.

The Field Bag

If you plan on being out for the day, you should plan on bringing enough with you to stay out for the night just in case you need to. Here are the essential items you should have in your field bag:

1. **A cell phone with a solar charger.** Make sure your phone is fully charged when you set out but also take a charger. You can purchase a solar charger for around twenty dollars. Not only does it allow you to recharge with sunlight, it also serves as an energy bank and usually has an integrated LED flashlight as well. You want your cell phone in case of an emergency and so that you can check the weather periodically.

2. **A first aid kit.** It should include bandages, including an elastic bandage, gauze, cloth tape, a tourniquet, a small roll of duct tape, pain and anti-inflammatory medication, allergy medication, and tick-removing tweezers in addition to your personal preferences. Download the Red Cross First Aid App on your phone. If you are a few miles or more from help, any injury can become more serious, so be prepared to stabilize and treat an injury quickly.

3. **Water.** For a daylong excursion, take two liters of water with you. Also pack a few iodine tablets for treating water should you be out longer than expected and need to treat water for drinking. The LifeStraw brand offers a convenient alternative to iodine tablets. If you know that you're going to want a hot cup of coffee or tea or another warm drink while you're out, bring a packable pot for boiling water, which is another way to treat water.

4. **Extra food.** Always bring more food than you think you will need. Nuts, dried fruit, jerky, and protein bars are great options. The food we eat acts like a fire in our bodies that generates heat and energy. When out in the field, especially if you end up being out longer than you expected, or even overnight, you'll need fuel to throw on

the fire to help it burn all night long. Avoid high sugar foods, which are only good for a short burst of energy. A balance of complex carbohydrates and protein is ideal for sustaining energy.

5. **Emergency whistle.** Many backpacks today have whistles integrated into their sternum straps, which is brilliant. If you are ever lost or in trouble, an emergency whistle allows you to sound an alarm. It is much more energy efficient and effective than yelling. These whistles are inexpensive and available at outdoor equipment stores, online, and even at some gas-station convenience stores. Make sure you carry at least one in your field bag at all times.

6. **Field guide(s).** I traveled for years with a copy of my *Peterson Field Guide to North American Trees* always in my bag. That book is full of pressed leaves I picked up on my walks. It even holds the tail of a chipmunk I found under the perch of a red-tailed hawk! Depending on your interests—whether trees, birds, animal tracks, clouds, mushrooms, insects, etc.—bring a field guide or two or download their apps on your phone to keep your bag light. A guide is a great resource for observing nature. I still prefer opening a book to pulling out my phone, since I don't want to get pulled into distractions on my phone.

7. **A journal and a pen.** You'll want a durable journal and a pen for sketching, making notes, or simply writing down the experience you have while communing with the living earth. Spending reflective time outdoors can catalyze insights, ideas, memories, and other experiences that you feel compelled to document.

8. **A map and a compass.** A topographical map of the land you are on along with a baseplate compass for charting your route are useful for basic orientation. Of course, most phones now have a built-in compass, but having a physical compass and being able to use it with a physical map allows you to leave the phone safely stowed away. And they work when the phone runs out of power.

9. **A multi-tool.** I am a big fan of the multi-tool, which is similar to a Swiss Army knife. Most multi-tools today have pliers as the central function, with different blades, screwdrivers, bottle and can openers, files, wire cutters, and other tools. If you can, buy a high-quality multi-tool. There are a lot of cheap knockoffs, which I haven't found to be of much use in the field. You can use a multi-tool for foraging, shelter-building, fire making, cooking, and other tasks on a hike or around camp.

10. **A fire kit.** Every field bag should have a tool for making fire. Depending on your preference and skill level, it could include waterproof matches, a lighter, a ferrocerium rod and striker, flint, a steel and char cloth, a hand or bow drill kit, and tinder. (We will discuss the various ways to kindle fire later in this chapter.)

11. **A headlamp.** A good headlamp is essentially a flashlight attached to a headband. Flashlights are useful, but they are difficult to use when performing camp tasks or hiking at dusk when you want your hands free to maintain your balance on a trail. A headlamp allows you to put light where you need it while freeing both hands. You can also use a headlamp

to signal to other people if you ever get lost. Most come with an automatic flashing or SOS function.

12. **Extra clothes.** Additional layers, socks, gloves, and a hat are essential in your field bag. If you take a wrong step into a stream and get your feet and body wet, changing into dry clothes will keep you warm and protect you from hypothermia. In a pinch, you can also use extra socks as gloves.

13. **An emergency blanket.** Pack a reflective emergency blanket that will help you conserve body heat if you are out longer than expected. They are inexpensive, light, and easy to pack. They can also be used as a reflecting surface in an improvised shelter to help reflect the heat from your fire into your sleeping space.

14. **A tarp or a rain fly with cordage.** A compact tarp or a packable rain fly is the final essential piece of equipment in your field bag. You can use it to fashion shelter quickly so that you stay dry and out of the wind. You can tie up a lean-to shelter between small trees, or use a hiking pole as a center pole, staking the corners to the ground. In any case, you'll never regret having this item at the bottom of your bag when the need arises.

There are certainly many other items you could include in your field bag, like a small hatchet, a folding handsaw or pruning shears for making tools, a long-burning candle, a small hammock—but in my experience, these basic fourteen items are the most essential. As you spend more time outdoors, you'll customize your own essential list.

MEDITATION FOR ENTERING THE WILD

It's important to transition into a place of present-moment awareness before entering the more-than-human world. You don't want to plow through like a runaway train. Prepare to mentally downshift from the outcome-oriented and hyper-focused mental state we are often in. Shift to a slower, more receptive space to attune to the rhythms of the land and the creatures whose neighborhood you now will be entering.

Before embarking on a journey into a forest, meadow, or other wild space, take a few moments to center yourself. Pause. Close your eyes. Take a few slow, deep breaths. Let the exhalation be twice as long as the inhalation. Let go of whatever thoughts are rattling around in your head, whatever stress or worry you are transmitting. Empty your cup. Tune in to the sounds, sensations, and rhythms of the land all around you. Stretch out with your feelings and sense the life presence of the living earth. Know that the beings who call this land home are paying close attention to what is going on. They have to—their lives depend on it. Your presence will be felt, noticed, and communicated far and wide. Notice the birds and the chipmunks; notice the little creatures we sometimes think of as background noise. In a relaxed way, be curious, and with your eyes closed, notice everything that is happening around you. Take a few minutes to be with it all.

Then open your eyes and look around. Take some time to simply observe everything. Now take a moment to express your gratitude to the land. You may even ask permission of the earth for your time in this space, sending reverence to all the inhabitants. Enter the land with respect. Set a strong intention to stay present and connected with your breath and to create as little disturbance as possible. Let each footstep be an experience of soulful connection with the living earth, each breath a rite of interbeing with the holy winds that blow, with all life that shares the breath.

With time, this practice for entry will transform how you approach your time outdoors. You want to bring awareness to your rewilding, to be mindful of your surroundings and how you show up. In time you will grow into comfort and belonging on the land.

Fire, Our Friend in the Wild

Before television and touch screens, there was fire, our friend and comforter for millennia. In Sanskrit, the word for fire is *agni*, and it is the very first word written in the Vedas, the oldest sacred books in world literature. As I noted earlier, Hindus give the first word in their sacred texts special importance. To reflect on the word *agni* is to find the seed that contains all the wisdom of the Vedas.

Fire is central to human culture. Mastering the art of creating fire was a turning point in our evolution as a species, and this is reflected in the myths and legends of peoples all over the world. Fire gives both light and warmth. Fire allows us to cook our food and heat our shelters. By its very nature, it calls us into circle practice, as we instinctually gather around. Fire's mesmerizing display of color and light guides our awareness into a state of soft fascination, relieving fatigue and bringing us into a state of trance-like meditation. It also creates a perfect setting for bringing the day to a peaceful and collective conclusion. Fire guides us into a natural state of harmony and healing, individually and collectively.

Yet many people today live in places where making a natural fire may not be an option. Here are some simple options for bringing the element of fire into your life.

- **Candles.** Especially in the darker and colder months of the year, lighting candles can be a wonderful way to bring fire into your home. At the end of the day, consider turning off all of your electronic devices, lower the lights, and light a candle or two. Allow your senses to rest in the natural darkness. Gaze into the flickering flame of a candle and allow yourself to enjoy the simple beauty of its flame and the light. A candle is a miniature campfire. Candle meditation can help you drop into the present moment in a deep and meaningful way. A candle can also serve as a centerpiece for a family council or meeting, where everyone shares while enjoying the candlelight.

- **Incense and other sacred herbs.** Burning incense, aromatic herbs, or tree resins like frankincense and myrrh is another way to invite the fire element into your home and life. The burning ember releases both smoke and aroma, which can be stimulating to the mind and the spirit while soothing through your sense of smell. Sitting and gazing at the dancing smoke can also be a sweet meditation.

- **Fireplaces and woodstoves.** If you already have an indoor place for fires, then you can add meditation practices to your enjoyment of their warmth and light.

- **A screen fire.** In a pinch, another option is television fire, or "slow TV" as they call it in the Netherlands. Netflix, Amazon Prime, and YouTube all offer fire channels that make your television or handheld device a miniature fireplace. Although purists may scoff, I have found this to be a wonderful option when an actual fire just wasn't viable.

Smoke

Watching curls of smoke from incense or candles writhe and dance, especially on a cold, rainy afternoon, can draw us into the present. It's just a moment of peace, but it's also something more, something that arises from a certain kind of smoke. The smoke lifting off an incense stick and the smoke rising off a crackling fire of dry pine are a phenomenon of unique power and character. Smoke is so often dismissed as less than fire or just a byproduct. Yet smoke itself has a story. Smoke reveals the movement of the invisible air. Life-giving winds are given shape by smoke, like the invisible man who is suddenly revealed when covered with paint.

In the Lakota tradition, smoke is believed to carry the people's prayers skyward to the Great Spirit. Watching smoke dance is perhaps one of the most ancient forms of meditation. In monasteries and ashrams all over the world, incense is burned to clear negative energy, sanctify holy spaces, and brighten the mind for meditation. Smoke meditation can help us connect with the elements of air, space, and fire.

Guided Smoke Meditation

Light your favorite incense or make a small fire outdoors.
Then sit comfortably and slowly allow your breathing
to deepen. Let attention rest on the dancing flame or
smoldering red embers. Keep breathing consciously
until the mind begins to settle. Bring your attention
now to where the smoke lifts off the flame or ember.
Gaze at the ever-changing movement of the smoke.
Allow yourself to simply enjoy and be carried by the
rising, curling, dancing smoke. Whatever worries, fears,
concerns, or burdens you may be carrying, offer them
up. Whatever you may be feeling thankful for, let it rise.

If you have other prayers or deep desires in your heart, imagine them lifting off and being carried away on the wind. See your gratitude rising into the sky and being received by the cosmos, extending infinitely above you.

Fire 101

As a child, I watched a movie called *Quest for Fire*, about a small group of Neanderthals who encounter a community of early Homo sapiens for the first time. Unlike the Neanderthals, the humans had learned the art of creating fire, and the Neanderthals watch transfixed as a woman demonstrated the skill. She twirls a stick between her palms with its tip touching another piece of wood, first slowly and then faster and faster, until a thin wisp of smoke begins to emerge from the dust the friction creates. She bends down and gently blows on the small mound and then gently transfers it into a bundle of tinder. She keeps breathing into the tiny nest in her hands until the smoke begins to billow and suddenly a flame jumps out of her hands. Fire is born!

The look of total wonder on the Neanderthals' faces is the same look that students of the outdoors get when they see fire brought forth in this way today. It is the look I had on my face the first few times I witnessed this ancient human ritual. And it is a ritual. It must be done in a certain way, under certain conditions, and with a certain attitude. If everything is done in the right way, a transformation of heat, fuel, and oxygen happens—and it gets me every time. Some people who have seen me demonstrate this technique have wept. In our modern age especially, when few people carry lighters or matches anymore, to see fire brought into being the old way triggers a deep response. This skill connects us to our earliest ancestors. Every single human being has ancestors who knew and used this technique.

Learning how to make fire requires skill and responsibility. Fire can cause terrible destruction. Being a firekeeper, someone who creates, sustains, and works with fire respectfully and reverently, means making safety your number one priority. Know your local zoning rules and laws regarding fires. Pay attention to local fire warnings or bans.

Never make fire in dry windy conditions, and always have enough water on hand to completely douse any fire you make. Avoid making fires in places that do not have an existing fire scar. Be responsible, courteous, and aware when collecting fuel from the land, and always leave the land in better condition than you found it.

Fire requires three things: heat, fuel, and air. Heat comes from a match, lighter, spark, or friction. Fuel is tinder and kindling and larger pieces of wood. Tinder is tiny, dry material; twigs the width of pencil lead, the cambium (inner bark) from dead trees, and white-birch bark are all great tinder. Newspaper and dryer lint are also commonly used as tinder. Kindling is slightly larger material, usually twigs and sticks that are a little bigger than tinder. As you collect your material, stack the tinder and kindling in separate piles, so that you can feed your fire slowly. As the heat grows, you gradually add larger fuel. Once you have a good fire going with the kindling, you can add larger pieces of wood. You're not building a bonfire (which is not necessary and actually an inefficient waste of fuel).

The Tipi Fire

The most common and effective type of fire to build is called "a tipi fire," because it is shaped like a circular cone with the tinder at the base and kindling leaning against it in a circle, creating a tipi shape. Because heat rises, the incline of the tipi fire allows the fire to climb up the fuel to the peak, creating a natural and effective convection current. And in case of rain, the shape of a tipi fire allows fuel to shed falling water more effectively than other types of fires, such as the log-cabin style, in which the pieces of wood are arranged in a flattish, broad square. If you are new to making fires, I suggest you start your first one with matches. See if you can build your tinder and kindling in such a way that you can use only one match to get it going.

To make a fire with matches or a lighter, pile tinder at the base of your tipi and light it. Have your dry piles of gradually larger kindling prepared before you light your fire, so that as it grows, you can feed it slowly and steadily. And have the larger wood nearby to keep the fire going.

If you are making fire using a more traditional method, such as flint and steel or the bow drill, you will need to create a small tinder nest to hold your char cloth or to receive a spark. It is called "a nest" because the tinder material is rolled into a small ball and then kneaded, massaged, and shaped into a small circular nest with a depression in the exact center where the char cloth or coal is placed in order to protect and nurture it until the tinder ignites in a flame. A tinder nest can vary greatly in size, depending on the materials that are available. You will want to become familiar with tinder sources in your area. Good tinder is composed of fine, dry plant fibers, although you can also use lint from a dryer, as mentioned earlier, which is highly flammable. (That's why you should clean out your lint catcher as well as your dryer exhaust and duct, and never leave the house with the dryer running.)

Tipi fire

My favorite source of tinder is white-birch bark, which is highly flammable even when wet. The stringy inner bark of tulip trees is also excellent if it can be harvested from dead trees that have had a chance to start to dry out. The cambium of many trees can be peeled off and rubbed between the hands to loosen the fibers. But only peel bark off dead trees so that you do not injure living ones. The material can then be shaped into a nest. Simply press your thumb into the center of the compact bundle to create a central space for your flame or coal. If you are using dryer lint, you can place it in the middle of your nest or roll the lint itself into a nest. One of my favorite tricks is to wrap a thick strip of white-birch bark around my tinder nest in the same way you might see bacon wrapped around the outer edge of a filet. Once you light the nest, the ring of bark around the edge feeds off the tinder nest and provides good heat for the larger twigs you add.

A fire is like a baby: at first it needs small portions of easily digest-ible food, and then gradually it needs more food as it grows. The tinder nest provides the digestible fuel for your baby fire; it nurtures the ember that you will breathe into life and that ignites into flame. The tipi fire is a reliable and comforting fire, which you can master with just a little practice. Now let's explore some other fires that require a good deal more practice but that are worth the effort.

The Ferro (Ferrocerium) Rod

Ferrocerium is a metal alloy that is scraped to spark a fire without matches or a lighter. Ferro rods, as they are called, contain magnesium and a metal, such as iron or steel, and sometimes the rare earth metal cerium. When scraped with a knife blade or a piece of steel, the rod throws off sparks that can burn as hot as 3,000 degrees—hotter than the temperature of molten lava! Ferro rods can spark even when wet, and because of their sparks' high temperature, ferro rods are helpful for starting a fire in the rain.

If you decide to stock a ferro rod in your field bag, you might also take along a sealable plastic bag of dryer lint, which makes good tinder as it can easily catch a ferro spark and ignite. But a ferro rod can also ignite finely shredded white-birch bark, the dried cambium found underneath the bark of certain dead trees, as well as paper, cotton, shavings from resinous heartwood, and other tinder.

Arrange your tinder bundle, dryer lint, or other tinder on the ground, so that the sparks from the rod will fall into the nest. To throw sparks off a ferro rod, use the back of a knife blade. Please note that the back side of your blade must have a sharp right angle; otherwise, use a scraper designed specifically for a ferro rod. Once the spark ignites the tinder, add small twigs around the tinder in the tipi shape. As the twigs ignite, continue adding larger and larger pieces of wood until the fire is the size you want.

Flint and Steel

The ferro-rod method is different from the flint-and-steel method. Flint and steel do not involve the use of a ferro rod and are some-what more challenging. The spark from flint and steel is close to 800 degrees, about 2,000 degrees cooler than a spark from ferro. In the flint-and-steel method, a high carbon-steel striker, which is shaped to wrap around the fingers (almost like brass knuckles) is struck against a piece of very hard stone, often flint of some kind. The hardness of the flint causes a very small shaving of steel to ignite and fly off into the air (the spark). Because this small spark is so much cooler than that created by a ferro rod, a material different from dryer lint is needed for tinder. We have to use something called "char cloth" to catch our spark.

Char cloth is made from cotton or linen that has been cut into small squares and cooked at a high temperature inside of a small tin (like the tin for breath mints) over a bed of hot coals for five to seven minutes. You can use an old tee shirt or a towel or jeans, but make sure that the fabric is all vegetable-based, with no synthetic material. Poke a small hole in the top of the tin with a hammer and nail or a knife, so that the smoke can escape as the cloth cooks and the tin doesn't explode as heat and pressure build up inside it. After five to seven minutes, when smoke is still coming out, take the tin out of the coals using tongs. Set it on a rock or somewhere safe where it won't ignite anything around it, and let it cool completely, until no more smoke is coming out, before you try to open it to retrieve the cloth. The cloth inside should be completely blackened or charred. If it's not all black, you might want to repeat the cooking for another five minutes. The char cloth might be somewhat fragile to the touch after cooking, although you don't want it to disintegrate. You need to handle it carefully and separate all the different pieces. You want to use only one at a time, but each char cloth will be ready to catch a spark.

Clear the space where you want to make your fire. Assemble the kindling and larger wood and arrange the kindling in a rough tipi that you can slip the tinder nest into once you have a flame going in the char cloth. Ready your tinder nest.

When you're ready to make the fire, place the char cloth on your tinder nest and strike your flint with your striker until a spark lands on the char cloth and begins to glow and smolder. This may take a little while as it is hard to control where a spark will fly. You may throw off a lot of sparks that go everywhere except onto your char cloth before one lands and catches. Also, pay attention to where the sparks fly in case you need to stomp any out. Once a spark lands on your cloth and catches, you have a little time and can relax. A piece of char can smolder for at least a few minutes before it burns up.

Once the cloth is smoldering, pick up the tinder nest, put it in the palm of your hand, and gently press the smoldering char cloth into the depression in the center of the nest. Wrap the nest around the smoldering char and gently breathe onto the nest until you begin to see smoke. Keep blowing until that smoke becomes steady and abundant, and then blow harder until that nest ignites into flame. Place your flame on the kindling and keep your fire by feeding it with small sticks. Congratulations! You just birthed fire using an ancient method.

Take a few deep breaths and invite gratitude for the gift of this fire. Take a few minutes to sit with your fire, gazing into the flames. Simply be with your fire and notice its effects on you. Fire can be a powerful doorway to meditation. When you are finished sitting, extinguish the fire with water, making certain all embers are completely out.

Fire Meditation

For our fire meditation, we build a very small fire that is intended to burn for only ten to fifteen minutes. The practice involves preparing, kindling, tending, and gazing into a small fire, and then allowing it to burn out completely on its own. We approach the creation, enjoyment, and passing of this living flame with reverence and respect. Most of the time during the fire meditation is spent gazing into the fire and allowing it to hold your focus. You may wish to speak to the fire, or you may want to place a prayer stick or a letting-go offering into the fire. You can imagine that the smoke is carrying your worries, prayers, or intentions. Here are the steps.

1. **Set an intention.** Before setting out to gather your tinder, kindling, and fuel, take a few deep breaths, close your eyes, and clear your mind. Turn off your phone and clear the next thirty minutes as sacred time with the element of fire. If you have a specific intention for your meditation, such as healing, forgiveness, letting go, or grieving, take a few moments to get clear about your goal.

2. **Take a walk to gather tinder, kindling, and fuel.** Pay attention as you go, and be aware of your surroundings. Move slowly and enjoy this simple task. You are outside, there is nowhere else you need to be and nothing else you need to be doing. Gather your fuel with reverence and gratitude.

Gather only fallen wood or harvest limbs that are dead so you do not harm a tree. Just a handful of small twigs, eight to sixteen should suffice.

3. **Prepare your tinder bundle and separate your fuel into little piles.** Engage in this practice as you would a Japanese tea ceremony. Let the simple task of sorting absorb your attention.

4. **Take a few moments to connect with gratitude.** Ask for the gift of fire. Feel your connection to the long line of firekeepers who came before you. To be a firekeeper is to carry the hope of humankind. Kindle your tinder bundle with a bow drill, hand drill, flint and steel, or ferro rod. Give thanks.

5. **Begin fire gazing.** Take this time now to be present with the living, breathing fire. Feed it and allow your awareness to be absorbed in its light and movement. Allow the fire to teach you. Be open to what comes.

6. **Allow the fire to die.** Do not interfere with the natural way in which the fire burns through its fuel. Allow this natural process to unfold. Stay with your fire after the flame has gone out. Feel the heat still radiating from the coals. Be with the fire until no more smoke rises. In your own way, say thank you to the fire, and then gently and respectfully pour water or lay snow onto the cooling embers.

The Bow Drill

The bow drill is a technique for making fire with friction. You may have seen drawings of the tools in scouting manuals or basic survival books, although the details of exactly how to fashion a proper kit are often missing. Even if you have all the proper pieces and know how to use them, making a fire using this technique can still be challenging. In fact, I find that friction-fire practice is profoundly humbling. When I am gifted with a coal—a tiny, burning ember of wood dust that I then breathe into a leaping flame—the experience is made sweeter by the sweat equity and the sacrifice involved. A sacred fire, brought into being through the friction method, is not the same kind of fire as one brought forth with a lighter or match. It has a

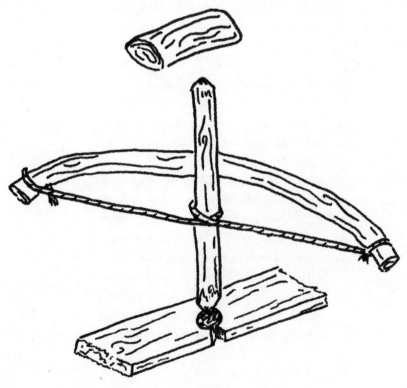

Bow drill

greater presence, meaning, and value to you, who brought it forth with humility and gratitude.

The bow drill has four components: a fire bow, hearthboard, spindle, and handhold.

- **The fire bow** is a bent piece of wood with cordage attached to each end. The length of the bow should be approximately from your armpit to your wrist. The cordage is wrapped around the spindle and used to turn it round and round, back and forth. This action creates intense friction between the spindle and the hearthboard.

- **The hearthboard** is a rectangular piece of wood with a pie-shaped wedge carved into the face of it. The spindle will grind down into this depression and create wood dust. The pie-shaped wedge collects and holds the wood dust, which eventually ignites into a coal.

- **The spindle** is a wooden rod about as wide as your thumb and as long as the space from the tip of your thumb to your pinkie finger when making the "hang-loose" sign. The spindle is turned by the back-and-forth motion of the bow, and it is the heat generated by the friction between the tip of the spindle and the hearthboard that creates the coal.

- **The handhold** is a stone or a piece of bone or wood that you use to press down on the spindle while turning it with the bow. The handhold keeps the spindle in place and protects your hand from the heat being generated. The point of contact between the top of the spindle and the handhold should be lubricated with sweat, ear wax, crushed pine needles, or other body oils to prevent excessive friction. You do not want to make a coal at the top of the spindle.

The bow- and hand-drill techniques are effective for making fire, of course, but they are also disciplines that have much to teach us about life. The spindle could be understood to represent male energy, the hearthboard female energy, and the coal the life that is created through the friction of male and female. To bring a coal to life requires passion, focus, skill, and stamina. Once a coal is born, you need to carefully and tenderly deposit the ember into a safe, supported nest of tinder. Then you blow ever so gently on that little coal, holding it in the nourishment of the fuel that it needs to grow into a dancing, living flame. This is the wonder of making a fire through friction. The lessons, healing, and meaning will differ for each person, but everyone I have ever seen make fire in this way—or even watch it being made—has been deeply moved.

The Hand Drill

The hand drill is another ancient tool for starting a fire through friction. It has two simple parts: a hearthboard, which is a flat, thin piece of wood, and a spindle, which is a narrow stick about 18 to 24 inches long. Like the hearthboard for the bow drill, the hand-drill hearthboard has a place where the tip of the spindle rests and a pie-shaped wedge cut out where the wood dust that is churned out by the spinning of the spindle gathers and eventually ignites into a small, delicate coal or ember. The spindle is a narrow stick about 18 to 24 inches long, which is turned in place by rubbing it rapidly between the palms of your hands until the wood dust smokes and then ignites.

The hand drill has a certain elegance in its simplicity, but it is more difficult to master than the bow drill. The tool itself is light and easy to transport. Also, if you are ever in a survival situation, you can make a hand drill more easily than a bow drill. Yet because the hand drill is challenging, many people never try it, or they tend to give up after a few failed attempts. I myself often thought that the technique was beyond my ability, even after I had made a few coals with a bow drill. Something about the hand drill just seems unattainable, but I choose to keep at it.

To practice the art of fire-starting, especially with a hand drill, is to become a student to something old and sturdy. The latest iPhone or other technological gadget is only relevant for a few years and then becomes outdated or irrelevant—but the hand drill abides. What other technology is as old or as useful? In the end, fire is essential. A fire is a friend to keep you company and give comfort in the dark of night. It keeps us warm in the depths of winter and cooks the food that fills our bellies. Fire has long been the focal point of community

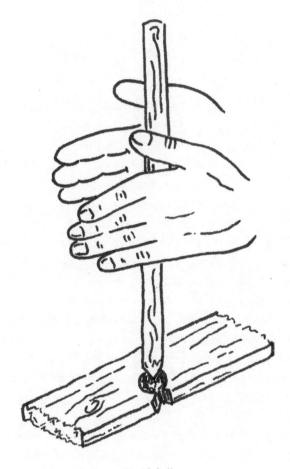

Hand drill

gatherings and the center of council circles. Around the fire is where our stories have been told, tales of the day's hunt and the great imaginings of how things came to be.

Our fire now is in our technology, which provides what we need to survive day to day but doesn't give us all that we truly need. The crackle of a good small fire and the voice of the wind in the trees is a medicine that only the earth can provide. Tom Brown Jr. always teaches that before we endeavor to bring forth fire in the sacred way, we start in a place of gratitude. So here is a meditation to center you for this creative act.

Gratitude Meditation for Birthing Fire

This life is a gift. Take a deep breath, and as you exhale, clear your mind. Let go of your agendas, plans, stories, opinions, and all the other stuff flying around in your mind. Take another deep breath and let it go. You are endeavoring to bring forth fire in the ancient and sacred way. Fire is a gift from the gods, from the spirits of the land. This way has been passed down for a long time. By practicing this ancient art, you are connecting to one of the deepest legacies in human ancestry. Allow yourself to be in this moment. You are in this eternal present moment that all people have been in. This is the same moment in which your ancestors brought forth fire. There is nowhere else to be and nothing else to do. Allow yourself to be here in this moment.

What do you hear? What can you feel?

Take a moment and give thanks for the gift of this breath. You are alive. Give thanks for your life. Take a few moments and give thanks for whatever comes to mind. If you can, speak words of thanksgiving aloud. If you have a deity or a language for speaking with what you consider to be divine, take this time to pray in your own way.

Let go of your intention to bring forth fire. Let go of any outcomes. Endeavor to undertake this simple and profound practice with humility and patience.

I tend to get pretty excited and pumped up about these skills. But sometimes I get so focused on the outcome of the skill that I lose track of the process. It's like that with so many things in life, isn't it? We focus on the money we are trying to make to buy the thing we want in the future, and in so doing, we miss the gift of the present moment, which is the only thing we ever actually have. Working with bow and hand drill is one of my favorite practices, but sometimes when I get to working on making a coal, I strive and strive for something like fifteen minutes, until I realize I haven't been in a state of gratitude. And if I'm not in a state of gratitude, I haven't been conscious of my breathing; instead, I've been contracted and tense, trying to force the process.

Recently I was in the woods sitting under one of my favorite trees working on a hand drill. I wasn't getting even a wisp of smoke. When I finally realized that I wasn't in a space of gratitude, I stopped what I was doing and centered myself. I started over again, and this time I stayed with my breathing, slowed down, and stayed very present with what I was doing. I began saying thank you out loud. Before long, I was thanking everyone who came to mind—old friends, my parents, my children, my wife, my siblings, the earth and the trees, the sun and the stars, my holy spirit. I found myself shifting to a treasured, old, sacred chant. The hand drill became a meditation. My mind was melting into my hands, into the spindle and hearthboard, and my mind was becoming purified by the intense focus. Smoke began to rise from the wood dust gathering around the base of the spindle. I kept working but eventually became tired and had to stop. I looked at my watch; thirty minutes had passed. I was covered in sweat.

I had not made a coal, but I didn't care. I felt good. I had lost track of time and my mind. I had found the now. I realized something that day. Or maybe I should say that I re-realized something, something I had forgotten. With these skills, it's not always about making fire but about getting to the place within yourself where you become the fire. It's the work of becoming empty, of honing your physical skills and your mental skills to the point where you cease to be a creature made up of different working pieces and instead become a unified consciousness, capable of bringing forth life and untold creative wonders. Like the fire born out of a churning of spindle on a hearthboard, the light of our own burnished awareness is the true gift of these skills. This means that the practicality of the hand drill is but one of the layers of this technique. It feeds the body, mind, and soul.

Shelter

Improvising a shelter that can keep you warm and dry enough to survive outdoors on a cold night is a valuable skill. If they found themselves in such a situation, few people today would know where to begin. Knowing how to make your own shelter for sleeping outdoors will improve your experience in the wild. Our modern houses create such a comfortable indoor environment that it is easy for people not to go outside at all. But indoor environments dysregulate our circadian rhythms, cutting us off from natural sunlight during the day and bombarding us with artificial light at night. (It's a good idea to try to phase out screen use after eight o'clock at night so that you can allow your body to begin winding down more naturally.) Camping for a few nights has been shown to be an effective intervention for resetting circadian rhythms and improving sleep.

Here are a couple of shelters everyone should know how to make because they require few tools or other man-made objects.

Debris Hut

Anyone can construct this simple design, which acts as both a shelter and a sleeping bag in one. I learned this technique at the Tom Brown Jr. Tracker School, in the Pine Barrens of New Jersey. It was inspired by the nests that squirrels make out of sticks and leaves. One of the great things about the debris hut is that you are essentially sleeping inside of a big pile of leaves. This, in itself, is incredibly stimulating for the senses.

Here's how it works. You will need one long ridge pole and many shorter sticks of varied lengths. The ridge pole should be a branch or a small fallen tree trunk or sapling, about a foot longer than you are tall. One end of this pole will rest on the ground, and the other will lean against a tree or a rock so that it is about three feet off the ground. If there's no rock or tree that high, find a three-and-a-half-foot stick with a cleft or Y shape at one end that can hold up the ridge pole. Sharpen the other end and push it several inches into the ground so that it will stay upright.

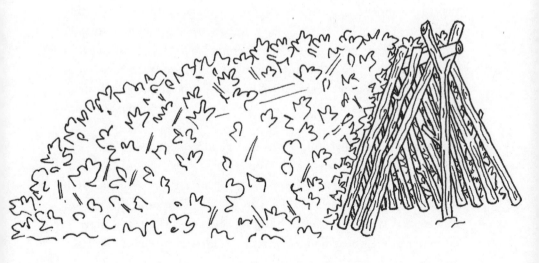

Debris hut

Once you have your ridge pole in place, you lean other, shorter sticks on a slant along both sides of the ridge pole to create a frame that forms a sheltered tunnel underneath. Each stick needs to be touching its neighbor as closely as possible, making a matrix that is close together so that leaves can't fall through it. If you're using a stump or rock instead of a Y-shaped stick, make sure to leave yourself an opening at that end, through which you can slide into the shelter. You can weave small sticks or vines horizontally through the slanted walls of sticks to create a basketlike appearance.

Once the frame is done, gather up enough leaves, boughs with needles, mosses, and other debris to cover your framed shelter completely. The leaves and other materials should be five- to seven-feet deep all around your shelter. The leaves will shed any water that falls if it rains and will trap in your body heat as well.

Now, gather pine boughs, if they are available, and lay them inside the shelter as a layer between your body and the earth. If you are lying directly on the cold ground, your body heat will be drawn out of you by conduction, so an insulating layer between you and the earth is essential. If you don't have pine boughs, just fill the shelter with more leaves and crawl in and out until you have compressed the leaves under you to create a natural pallet. Continue to fill the shelter with more leaves, until the whole cavity is completely stuffed, which in effect insulates you like a sleeping bag. If you have an extra canvas bag, shirt, or other piece of cloth, fill that with leaves, too. When it's time to sleep, crawl into the stuffing, pulling the leaf-filled shirt over the opening to create a door to help keep the heat in, and get cozy.

Sleeping in a debris hut is an unforgettable experience that connects you with the living earth. You lie in the embrace of the land, asleep in a fragrant nest. You may wake up on a frosty morning and stick your head out of your shelter to see the rising sun reflected off ice crystals. With this shelter-building skill, you will always have a place to rest your head and stay warm, whether in a pinch or because you want to draw closer to nature.

Quinzhee

The quinzhee is a winter shelter made out of snow, yet it stays above freezing inside, even when the temperature outside is below freezing. The word comes from the Athabascan language, but quinzhees were made by many peoples who lived in the northern latitudes and had to create temporary snow shelters.

If you're going to be hiking where conditions may get snowy, you will want to pack a foldable camp or snow shovel, which will make building a shelter much easier. To build a quinzhee, you need to make a big pile of snow, big enough for you and anyone else who is with you to fit under. Generally, about eight feet around and at least five feet high will do it.

If you can find a snowbank or big drift, you won't need to create as big a pile of snow. If a snowbank is not available, you will need to gather snow and create your pile. This can be a lot of work, and if you don't have a snow shovel or trowel, you will need to improvise. Snowshoes can be used as makeshift shovels. If you have an extra coat, blanket, tarp, or sleeping bag, they can be used for moving snow. You will need to use

Quinzhee, or snow shelter

your hands and arms to push snow into your receptacle and then carry or drag your snow to your pile.

Once you have made your pile, you need to let it rest for at least an hour so that the snow compresses enough so that it is stable and you can carve into it. While you're waiting for the snow to set, collect at least thirty sticks that are at least a foot long. Once the snow has set, you will push the sticks into the walls of the quinzhee, all around the outside, top, and sides, so that only an inch of each stick is poking outside of the quinzhee. These sticks will help you know how much snow to clear out of the inside of your pile, and they will help you keep the roof and walls at least a foot thick all around.

On the side of the snow pile that is away from the prevailing wind, begin digging into the pile to create an entrance and to hollow out the inside. If you do not have a shovel or trowel, you can use a stick to break up the snow and then use your hands to hollow out and smooth the space inside the quinzhee. Whenever you hit the end of a wall stick, stop digging there and dig toward the next stick. Do not expose more than the end of any stick because the ceiling and walls will be thin and lose strength.

Mark the entrance with an upright stick or flag so that you can find it if you leave the quinzhee and it snows or the wind blows snow drifts over it. The marker will also be a sign to anyone outside if you become trapped inside. If you have a shovel, keep it inside with you should you need to dig out.

Once you are finished hollowing out your shelter's walls, you can create a channel in the snow on the floor that runs from the entrance to the back wall to make two snow beds. Clear the channel all the way down to the bare earth. It will act as a funnel for cold air, which will drop and run out the door. When you are finished, poke a small ventilation hole in the ceiling.

Before you crawl into your quinzhee, you may be able to find a slab of frozen snow or ice to pull over the entrance after you enter as an improvised door and windscreen.

Sleeping in a sheltered pile of leaves or in a snow cave reminds us that we, too, are animals and that we can exist in a more immediate and direct contact with the earth than we normally think possible. These experiences break down the walls that separate us from the more-than-human world and can help to reframe our ideas and beliefs about what is necessary for fulfillment and happiness. Sleeping in shelters is akin to walking barefoot on the earth. Both practices help us explore and expand our comfort zones and reestablish contact with the wilder parts of ourselves.

But now ask the beasts, and let them teach you;
and the birds of the heavens, and let them tell you.
Or speak to the earth, and let it teach you.

JOB 12:7–8

5

OUT OF EXILE

Skills for Coming Home to the Living Earth

My wife, Elaina, is a professional photographer. She was shooting a family reunion at an apple orchard, and the patriarch of the family, a man in his seventies who lived in New York City, was puzzled when my wife encouraged them to pick and eat the apples off the tree, so she could get some action images.

The man asked her, "What do you do? Do you just pick them and eat them? Are they okay to eat?"

My wife assured them that the apples were really good and safe to eat. The man explained that he wasn't used to seeing food growing on trees.

When Elaina told me this story, I thought, *This is what disconnection from nature can look like*. Even a tradition as American as picking apples has become, in some places, a distant memory.

A hundred years ago, the world was less populated, and most people were involved in growing or procuring food. Whether tending animals, raising vegetables, or hunting, they had some connection to the source of their food. With the mass migration from the countryside to cities and the growth of industrial farming, fewer and fewer people know where food comes from. Part of rewilding is connecting with our food and getting involved in procuring it in mindful, sustainable, and direct ways.

Impermanence, Again

One of the fruits of mindfulness is an awareness of life's impermanence. Seasons come and go, people come and go, and life comes and goes. Meditation rests on the practice of establishing the seat of the observer, or witness, and being with life's ups and downs. Attachment to pleasure and aversion to pain are a natural response to living in a body; all living beings try to avoid pain and prolong pleasure. Nevertheless, all living creatures, by the very nature of their existence, must consume other living things to stay alive. If you contemplate the cycles of life regularly, then you live knowing that all living beings will one day die and that their bodies will become part of the cycle of life from which they originally arose. To live with this awareness changes your relationship to food, from viewing it as the means to acquire energy for survival, to viewing it as a sacred rite that affirms the way all life is connected. There is a reciprocity to be understood within the larger cycle of time, in which we, too, become part of the food chain when we die.

To bring rewilding to food is to practice gratitude for the gifts of this earth that sustain us and to make conscious choices so that what and how we eat sustains the greater good as much as possible. Foraging is the practice of gathering up the food that grows on the land where we live. Most of the time, the foods that we forage are wild, growing without human support. Picking is a little like foraging, except that when we pick apples or peaches or pumpkins, for example, we gather food that farmers have cultivated in orchards and fields.

When foraging for wild foods, we need to follow some ethical guidelines so that our presence on the land increases diversity and abundance rather than decreasing it.

1. For your own safety, never harvest anything you cannot identify with 100 percent certainty.

2. Never overharvest. Always leave plenty of whatever you are foraging.

3. Never forage in polluted areas or beside roads.

4. Leave no trace. Walk carefully and do not trample. Leave places where you forage well-tended and cared for.

5. Be a steward. Do not forage for species that are endangered or in low number.

Foraging and Eating by Season

Each season brings with it sights, smells, textures, sounds, and flavors that create new memories and remind us of years gone by. The circular rhythm of the seasons grounds us as we naturally attune to them in our daily habits, sleep, and diet. We still feel an innate urge to eat with the seasons, enjoying the foods that the land offers up. We crave warm, rich, hearty foods in the cold days of winter and lighter, cooling fare like salads and fruit in the hot days of summer. Some people do tend to eat the same kind of food all year long, feasting often rather than in the fall when the harvest arrives, which can set them up for weight problems, heart disease, diabetes, and even depression, since food affects mood. Spring was traditionally a time of fasting, not because a health coach said it should be but because the store of winter food was gone and there was little left to eat. Today, eating with the seasons is coming back, and we know that eating locally is good for our health as well as the planet's.

When life was intimately connected with food, the land, and the seasons, many ancient agrarian cultures honored the cycles of the year with cardinal points and holy days around the solstices and equinoxes as well as cross-quarter days, the halfway points between solstices and equinoxes. Christianity subsumed ancient pagan holy days by placing Christmas near the winter solstice, Easter near the spring equinox, and Halloween near the fall equinox. As we have become less connected to the land and our food sources, the origin of these seasonal markers has been obscured and, in some cases, commercialized, yet they still remind us of our planet's yearly journey around the sun.

My favorite practice for attuning to the food cycles of my bioregion is to forage for food growing naturally on the land. To me foraging is more than acquiring food; it is a way to commune with the generative forces of nature. Like the reciprocal bond in our breathing, in which the life-giving air of the earth is taken into our bodies and assimilated before it is offered back through our exhalation, foraging brings the earth to our bodies in deep and nourishing ways. The physical nutrition energizes and sustains us, and we also receive something else, an embodied connection with the trees, soil, plants, and water that provide this food to us.

At the Kripalu School of Mindful Outdoor Leadership, the guides-in-training go through seven days of mindful immersion in our forest classroom. Afterward, we all participate in a pine-needle tea ceremony. Each participant forages for a sprig of hemlock pine tree or white pine needles and brings these back to the base camp, where we have a pot of water boiling over a fire. They gently massage the needles or sprigs in their hands to release the oils and then hold the needles up to their noses and take deep breaths. As they inhale the essential oils of evergreen, they are transported by memory. Then, one by one, each person walks up to the cauldron of boiling water and drops their needles into it to create a tea. Someone takes the pot off the fire to let the needles steep, and then everyone gets a cup of forest tea. We hold it, inhaling and focusing our attention on the aroma of the pine-needle tea. Then we sip the tea. We all experience a deep union with the trees. Through this simple tea ceremony, the forest, the sacred space in which we have been immersed for days, enters the temples of our bodies. We are in the forest, and the forest is in us.

The following section on mindful foraging is organized by season. I also share a few of the wild foods I enjoy foraging in western Massachusetts. Take these as inspiration and as examples of what you might be able to find where you live. Every region is different and has its own local food.

Spring: Dandelion Greens, Wild Onions, Garlic Mustard, Fiddleheads, and Eastern Hemlock Shoots

Dandelions *(Taraxacum)*. In the early spring, one of the first things to grow up out of the still cold earth is the dandelion. Considered a weed by many homeowners and the petrochemical industry, the dandelion is one of the most abundant food sources we have. Every part of the plant is edible, and this hardy green is a powerful detoxifier, particularly of the intestines and liver. After eating the rich, heavy foods of winter, eating dandelion greens and flowers is a great way to clean out and prepare the gut for the return of all the abundant fresh foods of warmer weather.

I like to pick a whole bunch of young leaves and flower buds and bring them home to cook or to use raw in a salad. I wash them, then sauté them in olive oil, minced garlic, and salt. You can parboil the unopened flower buds for just a minute or two and then drain and eat them as is, or you can sauté the buds with the leaves. They are

Dandelion greens

delicious! After they open, the yellow flowers are a little more bitter, but you can make a tempura batter and fry them in oil to make fritters. You could also simply sauté them in oil or eat them raw. The bitterness in the leaves and flowers increases through the spring and summer, so they taste best in early spring, before the flowers open.

Once you experience the delicious abundance of the common dandelion, you will never look at a lawn the same again. If you are ever in a situation where food is scarce, the dandelion is your friend. But remember: you don't want to harvest dandelions from a lawn that has been treated with chemicals.

Wild Onions, or Ramps *(Allium tricocum)*. I am fortunate to live at the base of a mountain that is covered in wild onions, or what we call "ramps." From late winter into early spring, the ramp is one

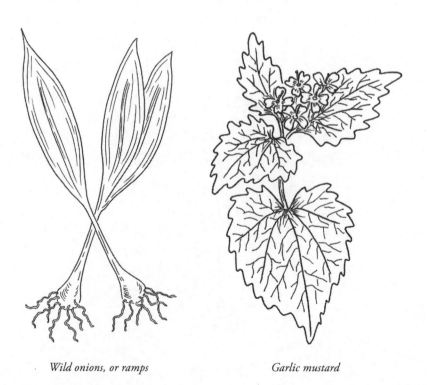

Wild onions, or ramps   *Garlic mustard*

of the first green shoots to poke out of the melting snow. The first ramp shoots let me know spring has truly arrived. Like other onions, these wild ones grow from a bulb underground. The base of a ramp is white with a slight pink hue. The part you eat above the base forms into green, wide, spear-shaped leaves. I cut them off just above the ground—never pull them up by the roots—and fill up a small shopping bag. If you harvest ramps, be sure to leave the bulbs in the ground so they can keep growing and be found again next year. I make sure that I don't overharvest and always leave about 80 percent of the ramps in any given patch.

Ramps have a delicious, mild, onion-like flavor. You can sauté them on their own or with the dandelion greens and flowers you harvested to enjoy a true foraged spring meal. You can also sauté them and fold them into an omelet, chop and add them to soups, sprinkle them on pizza, and even make a pesto with them.

Wild foods like ramps are healthful and precious. Unfortunately, in some places, ramps have been harvested so heavily that the old ramp beds are disappearing. So, if you find wild ramps on your land or in a public place, keep an eye on them. Be discerning about whether you should take any at all. If you can, be an advocate for them and raise awareness about sustainable foraging and conservation.

Garlic Mustard (*Alliaria petiolata*). Garlic mustard is an invasive weed that grows in abundance in New England and other parts of the country. Yet it is also delicious and highly nutritious. It crowds out native species, so you can feel good about harvesting this plant—it doesn't look like we're ever going to run out of it. Garlic mustard is easy to identify. It grows two to three feet tall and has alternate leaves. The leaves that grow near the bottom of the plant are heart shaped with scalloped edges that become pointier as they grow toward the top, where a cluster of small white flowers emerges. The leaves, which are the main edible part of the plant, tend to taste better (less bitter) if harvested before the flowers bloom. Garlic mustard leaves can be eaten in salads, used as a garnish, or in place of lettuce on a sandwich. You can also make a delicious pesto out of them. I love to sauté garlic mustard leaves with dandelion greens, ramps, olive oil, minced garlic, and a touch of salt. Delish!

Fiddleheads *(Matteuccia struthiopteris).* Fiddleheads are the unopened leaves of ferns in early spring. Nearly all ferns have fiddleheads, but it's the tops of the ostrich fern that you want to harvest, as not all fiddleheads are edible. Ostrich fern is an abundant native species in North America. Fiddleheads are easy to identify, although the window for harvesting is small, usually in late April or early May where I live in Massachusetts. I know a few places where they grow in abundance, and heading out on a Sunday afternoon to gather them is one of the great joys of spring for our family.

The fiddleheads themselves are coiled up in a circle about the size of a quarter and are good for harvesting when they are about two to four inches off the ground. Fiddleheads can be identified by the following characteristics: they have a bright green stem with a deep green groove on the inner side and a brown, feathery, paperlike material covering the head, which begins to fall off as they grow. There is at least one fern,

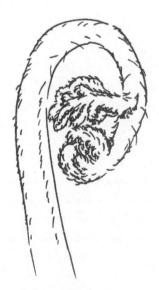

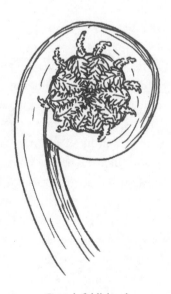

Bracken fiddlehead   *Ostrich fiddlehead*

bracken, which looks similar, but it is toxic—so it is best to go with an experienced forager your first few times out.

To prepare fiddleheads, rinse them thoroughly with cold water in a colander and pick off any of the brown papery material. Boil or steam them for ten minutes. You can eat them with butter and salt, or add them to a sautéed dish of mushrooms or other vegetables. Just remember to always boil them before you sauté them. Fiddleheads have a mild flavor, a bit earthy, somewhere between spinach and broccoli. I like to toss some fresh ramps in with my cooked fiddleheads, since they both come up around the same time.

Eastern Hemlock *(Tsuga canadensis)*. Another spring favorite for delicious foraging comes from the eastern hemlock tree. These beautiful and elegant conifers have flat, short needles that are dark green on top with two blue-white lines running the length of their underside. In the springtime, the eastern hemlock produces bright green needle tips that are soft and edible. You will notice them as you hike through the forest because the tips are so much lighter and brighter than the older

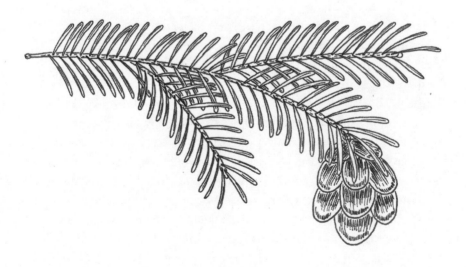

Eastern hemlock

needles on the trees. While hiking, you can pick and nibble them as you stroll under the watchful and gentle boughs of these beautiful trees. Close your eyes and say a few words of gratitude to the tree before and after you harvest its new growth.

The young needles have a lemony flavor and are high in chlorophyll, tannins, and vitamin C, which has antioxidant properties. In other seasons, the needles can be made into a tea. Choose a couple of tiny twigs, about the length of your index finger, and before steeping the needles, rub them between your hands to release the aromatic oils. Then cup your hands and bring them up to your nose to inhale the aromatic oils. Drop the needles into water that has been boiled and let them steep for five to ten minutes. You might want to strain the needles before you drink the tea, but you can also use your teeth to strain them as you drink. After a mindful stroll through the forest, a cup of hemlock tea is a beautiful way to bring the essence of the forest into the body and to awaken the sense of both taste and smell.

You may have heard of poison hemlock, an infusion that is credited with killing Socrates. But poison hemlock is not an evergreen tree like the eastern hemlock. Poison hemlock is an herbaceous plant without needles; it sprouts white flowers that look a little like Queen Anne's Lace. You cannot confuse the herbaceous hemlock plant with eastern hemlock tree needles.

There are many other delicious and nutritious plants to forage in the spring. I recommend getting a field guide or app to learn about them. You can also take a picture of a plant you're drawn to with your phone and find out from the internet if it's edible once you get home. Foraging is a way to reconnect with the wild, free, and abundant foods all around you, and it provides a powerful shift in perspective. You see that the living earth is abundant. A single oak tree can produce thousands of acorns, while a wide-open lawn can contain thousands of blooming dandelions. Many people who believe that food and resources are scarce overlook the abundance of nature's bounty. What a joy it is to receive the nutrition that the earth provides for us each and every day. A sip of hemlock tea, a dish of sautéed dandelion, and a piece of sourdough bread spread with ramp pesto can teach us an important lesson: the earth loves us and wants us to be happy!

Summer: Wood Sorrel, Staghorn Sumac, and Wild Blueberries

Wood Sorrel *(Oxalis)*. The wood sorrel is one of the most adorable plants growing on the earth. It is widespread, so you can find it in almost any yard. Wood sorrel is a small weed with three heart-shaped leaves and a small yellow flower when it blooms. Sometimes wood sorrel is mistaken for clover, which is also edible. The wood sorrel's heart-shaped leaves have a tart, lemony flavor. You can nibble the leaves raw or sprinkle them on salads, soups, fish, or pasta. It is one of my favorite wild edibles, and it is the first one I taught my children to pick. My daughter, Cora, loves to find what she calls "lemon clover."

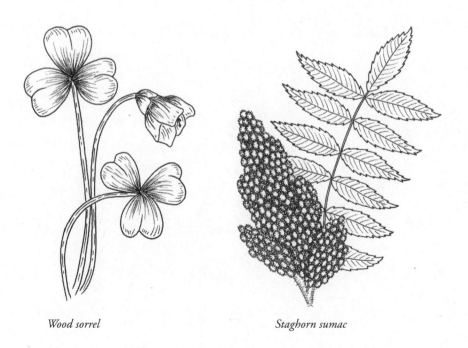

Wood sorrel   *Staghorn sumac*

Staghorn Sumac *(Rhus typhina)*. Staghorn sumac is a native shrub in New England that is found in sandy or rocky soil. It is not to be confused with poison sumac, which has greyish-white berries that grow and hang down in clusters. Staghorn sumac produces large, deep red berry clusters that point up to the sky, and its branches have a velvety surface, like that on newly grown deer antlers. Staghorn sumac often grows in disturbed areas, open lots, and along fences and the edges of open spaces. The red berry clusters can be picked in late summer and soaked in cool water to make a pink "sumac-ade," a delicious tart beverage that tastes a lot like lemonade. The berry cones contain a lot of vitamin C. You only need to soak the berry clusters for five to fifteen minutes for the water to be infused by both the color and flavor of the berries. The longer the berries soak, the more sumac flavor. You can add your favorite sweetener to taste. I prefer maple syrup and like to drink my sumac-ade over ice. This was a staple drink in New England for hundreds of years, before imported lemons became widely available. Because sumac is such an easy plant to identify, forage, and prepare, it is another great food to forage for beginners and children.

Wild Blueberries *(Vaccinium angustifolium)*. Wild blueberry can be found on well-drained, sandy, highly acidic soils. In western

Wild blueberries

Massachusetts, I often find it on mountaintops and hills along my favorite hiking trails or growing near the edges of ponds and lakes. There is nothing quite so fine to forage as you stroll through the woods on a hot summer day as the delicious and highly nutritious wild blueberry. The lowbush blueberry is usually a short bush with small, dark green leaves in summer that turn brilliant orange and deep red in the fall. The berries are smaller than the cultivated berries sold in stores and dark blue in color. Extremely high in antioxidants, wild blueberries are considered a superfood.

At my house we planted two lowbush blueberries along with six highbush blueberry plants so that we'd have them growing near our home as well as up the mountain. My kids love going in the backyard every day in August to check on the crop and pick them for a snack. You might also have other kinds of wild berries near you. Blackberries and raspberries are also common throughout the United States. Both grow wild and have no poisonous look-alikes.

When my wife was in the early stages of labor with our daughter, Cora, we went blueberry picking at a local farm so she could be outside and moving around. Every August around Cora's birthday, we now go to that same place and pick blueberries. It's a sweet tradition that connects us to that special moment in our lives and the land on which it happened.

Berries are a seasonal, summer food. If you don't have wild blueberries near you, see if there are places where you can pay to pick. You can get a lot more berries for your money at a local farm that is open to the public than you can at the market.

Fall: Apples and Hickory Nuts

Apples *(Malus pumila)*. Fall is by far my favorite season. As someone who runs hot, I am often uncomfortable in the summer. I love when the first winds of autumn begin to blow, and I know I can look forward to cooler mornings, less heat and humidity, and wearing layers. Fall is also a time when many wild foods are ready for harvesting and the growing season comes to an end. In pagan cultures, the year draws to a close around the time of the autumn equinox, which is called "Samhain" in the ancient Celtic culture. Many fruits, vegetables, and tree nuts are harvested in the fall, the last chance to gather what is needed for the long dark of winter.

Picking apples outdoors in the fall is an easy way for people to dip their toes into sourcing food for themselves. Of course, picking apples cannot be considered wild foraging, as apple orchards are heavily managed. Pick-your-own farms, which are open to the public, grow many different varieties of apples in their orchards. What a wonderful feeling it is to get outside in the crisp autumn air, picking and eating apples, whose cool, crisp, and refreshing qualities reflect the characteristics of their season of harvest. Apples can be eaten off the tree, pressed into juice or cider, baked in pies, or cooked down for sauces and butters.

I've been foraging for a long time, and I still love spending an afternoon in late September picking apples with my family. It is truly quality time, away from the noise and stress of modern life, with only the sound of the wind and the colors of the earth for your entertainment. There is a purity and an innocence about picking, and conversation and spontaneous play rule the day. Like any kind of mindful time spent outside, sourcing your own food is nourishing on many levels. That you get to fill your home with the smell of apples and cinnamon baking is a wonderful benefit.

Hickory Nuts *(Carya ovata)*. Throughout my life I have been drawn to certain trees. One of my favorites is the shagbark hickory. When I was a kid, my dad would gather hickory limbs that fell on our land and chop them into chips, which he would use to slow cook and smoke pork shoulder. The smell of hickory smoke wafting on a warm breeze and the hickory-smoke flavor that seasoned the food were pretty special.

Hickory is a tough, strong tree. Its wood is very hard and dense, and it has long been used to make tool handles and baseball bats. Shagbark hickory bark peels off the tree trunks in long, vertical strips, giving the trees their shaggy appearance. Hickory trees produce nuts that fall to the ground in September and October. Of the different varieties of hickory trees, shagbark hickory nuts taste best. The nuts are oval, about an inch to two long and a little over a half inch to an inch wide. They're covered in a green casing that is sectioned in four quarters. When the nuts are ripe, the outer casing comes off easily. Hickory nuts are edible directly out of the shell and taste similar to a pecan or a walnut. They have a slightly sweet nutty flavor and can be used in place of either pecans or walnuts in your favorite recipes. Before almonds and other nuts grown in California were transported nationwide, gathering hickory nuts in the fall was a classic New England pastime. Hickory-nut pie was a staple on the Thanksgiving table of many New Englanders in the 1800s and early 1900s. Most people today have no idea that hickory nuts are an edible and abundant food source.

Every fall my kids and I enjoy at least one afternoon on a hickory-nut ramble. I know a few choice locations where big hickories drop lots of nuts. We bring canvas bags with us, as well as a few good rocks for breaking open the nuts. After we have collected a bunch, we like to sit down with our backs against the stable and comforting hickory trunks while we break open the nuts with our rocks. My daughter loves it. All the time kids are told not to be rough and not to break things, but kids love to smash stuff sometimes—and so do adults.

Hickory nuts

Wherever we go, my kids know they can gather hickory nuts and have food. They've also begun to develop a relationship with that life-giving tree. This is one of the great gifts of foraging, the way that intimacy with specific plant species brings us closer to the more-than-human world and allows us to perceive the great diversity of living things. Rather than seeing a sea of green or a blur of brown, we become aware and begin to differentiate the unique qualities of the different plant communities we share the earth with.

Winter: Jerusalem Artichoke, Wintergreen, and White Pine

Jerusalem Artichoke *(Helianthus tuberosus)*. A relative of the sunflower, Jerusalem artichoke is a native of eastern North America that has become naturalized in many other locations. First Nation peoples used

Jerusalem artichoke

it as a major food source. The edible part is the tuber, which stores its energy underground. The flowers are similar to sunflowers but smaller. Unlike sunflowers, Jerusalem artichoke tends to grow in patches. I have a patch of them in my backyard. Their stalks usually grow up to seven feet tall by the time late September comes around. You can harvest the tubers in the colder months, from late October through March, and eat them raw, roasted, steamed, boiled, or mashed. You can even make them into pasta, although I have never tried it myself. They have a crisp texture when eaten raw, similar to water chestnuts, and their flavor is similar to artichokes, which must be how they got the name.

Jerusalem artichoke is one of the best wild foods for winter foraging because, like potatoes, they provide a substantial meal that is delicious and filling. They are also a great comfort food, something you can throw in a roasting pan with other vegetables, fish, or meat for a tasty meal on a cold winter's night.

The one trick with Jerusalem artichoke is that they tend to be difficult to identify, especially in the middle of winter when the flowers are gone and the leaves have shriveled or blown away. One of the skills of foraging is remembering where edible plants are from one season to the next, when the food is ready to harvest. A stand of Jerusalem artichokes will come back year after year if you don't dig up all the tubers. They are incredibly resilient. Some home gardeners avoid growing them because they can be invasive.

Wintergreen *(Gaultheria procumbens)*. Winter in New England is cold, long, and often dark. The truth is, there is not much to forage in the wintertime in New England. Native American tribes who lived here before the European invasion lived off the stores from their fall harvest and summer hunting. When food grew scarce, they hunted deer, went ice fishing, and sometimes resorted to eating the inner bark of trees such as birch or hemlock.

But dotting the snow with tiny flecks of red on this stark beautiful landscape is a truly remarkable edible plant, the wintergreen. The wintergreen's small leaves have a dark green, leathery appearance. The wintergreen's berries are red, about the size of a pea. They mature in the fall, but their taste improves after being frozen. The leaves can be boiled to make a tea and also nibbled with their delicious berries. Wintergreen has a light, bright, refreshing flavor similar to black birch but slightly more minty. Wintergreen grows in low acid soils; I often find it near the tops of the ridges in the Berkshires, along some of my favorite hiking trails. There is something so simple and beautiful about the red and green of winterberry on a canvas of pure white snow.

Eastern White Pine *(Pinus strobus)*. In the depths of winter, the eastern white pine, like other evergreens, holds on to its green needles. Rich in vitamin C, like the eastern hemlock, the needles can be used to make a comforting tea. The eastern white pine is a prosperous and beautiful member of the forest community in New England. Its needles grow in packets of five, which is an easy way to identify it since *white* has five letters. The five needles of the white pine are also symbolic of the five nations of the Haudenosaunee (Iroquois) Confederacy, which chose the white

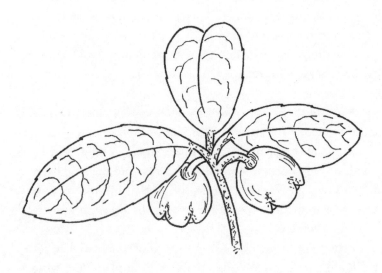

Wintergreen

pine to be the great "Tree of Peace." The weapons of the warring tribes are said to have been buried under the Tree of Peace when they joined together as one. The Iroquois culture and form of governance are known to have inspired our founders and the representative democracy they established for the United States.

To make a bright, citrus-pine-flavored tea from white pine needles, you will want to gather at least twenty packets of white pine needles. Rub a couple of the packets between your hands to release the pine resin, as you offer a gesture of thanks to the trees for this provision. You can drop the crushed needles into a pot of freshly boiled water and allow them to steep for five to fifteen minutes, although I like to cut them up into smaller pieces to help release the oils before steeping them. Strain the needles from the boiling water and pour the tea into a mug. Before sipping, hold the cup up near your nose and take a few deep inhalations. Drink as is or sweeten with maple syrup or honey. Enjoy!

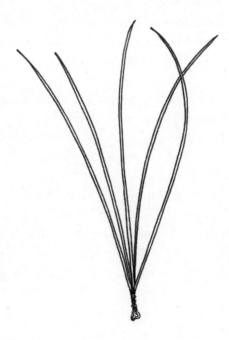

Eastern white pine

In the programs I lead, I often wait to introduce foraging until people have had a few days to relax and begin feeling comfortable on the land. Folks have a full seven days in our hemlock forest before they experience their first tea ceremony. They have been practicing mindfulness every day, often sitting against the trunk of a hemlock in the early morning, as they slow their breathing, take in the earth through all of their senses, and watch as a new day emerges from the night. Through this process, the trees, stones, and other members of the forest community become a part of their world, so on the seventh day, when we make hemlock tea and bring the essence of the forest into our bodies, the experience can be unexpectedly powerful.

During our first training, my co-trainer Mark turned to me in front of the group and handed me the first cup, which he invited me to offer to the forest. Honored and touched by his kind gesture, I took the cup and turned to look out at the forest. My eyes immediately landed on the bark of a shagbark hickory behind the tent we were gathered in. Though I had looked upon this tree many times and have a special affinity for hickories, this time I saw in the bark the face of an old, bearded man with a long nose. I was stunned, overcome with wonder and emotion. It felt to me in that moment that the forest was very much alive, aware, and awake to our presence, and that this was its way of saying thank you to us.

The intention that we set for all our practices, including rewilding, allows the practices to have the greatest impact. It's one thing to eat a berry or drink tea because you are hungry and thirsty, but it's another to recognize the miracle of a berry and the majesty of a tree and to invite their essence into communion with you. It is the consciousness we bring to our mindful rewilding that makes the difference between pure survival, man against nature, and true union, healing through intimacy with the great web of life that unites us all.

Tracking

Many people complain about the cold of winter, but I find that the landscape opens more fully to me in the winter months. Lush forests are easier to navigate after the leaves have fallen, and one can move more freely on the land without being bothered about ticks or mosquitoes. The woods behind my house is bordered by a small floodplain, which is practically impenetrable in summer. But in the winter, the undergrowth recedes, and I can traverse the wetland more easily. The marsh grasses and swamp trees provide a crucial habitat and sanctuary for many wild animals who live there year-round, including bobcats, deer, bears, foxes, coyotes, fishers, muskrats, raccoons, river otters, turkeys, and a whole host of birds who nest there each spring. In addition to the spaciousness of the land, the snow reveals the comings and goings of the more-than-human world as animals leave their tracks in the snow.

A few winters ago, when my son, Stryder, was just four years old, he and I went for one of our weekend walks in the woods behind our house. We crossed Coyote Bridge and the frozen marsh, making our way to the higher ground at the foot of the mountain, where we found two sets of very large, side-by-side coyote tracks. It was snowing that morning, and about a half inch had already fallen. These tracks were made in that newly fallen snow, which meant that these two large coyotes had moved through this area in the last thirty minutes or so. I told Stryder this and showed him the tracks. His eyes widened. I showed him how coyote tracks have four toe pads and how the back two toes tuck in close behind the front two. Coyote tracks tend to have a more oval shape than bobcat tracks. Stryder is eight years old now, and before we head out into the winter woods, we review the animal tracks I've taught him. I quiz him and his little sister, Cora. With time, both are becoming familiar with the tracks we see on the land, and I believe their familiarity with the presence of the more-than-human world supports their bond with our woodland friends.

In the spring, when the black bears emerge from their long winter slumber, we see their tracks in the muddy, wooded path next to our house. I've shown the kids that bear tracks have five toes, and anytime we find bear tracks, they look around and usually ask to go back in the house! Knowing that these large wild beings roam the land invokes a natural and necessary respect. Rather than clomping through the forest as if we were kings of the earth, we can acknowledge our wild relatives by acting with respect, humility, and an awareness of our place in the web of life.

Tracks tell us that even though we may not see animals moving on the land, they are out there, avoiding detection, blending into the shadows and wooded corridors that weave through the human world. Paying attention to animal tracks, signs, and scat is another way to reconnect with the wild.

The tracks or impressions that animals leave can be seen in mud, snow, sand, and leaf or pine litter. They make these impressions with their paws, hooves, bellies, snouts, tails, talons, and wings. Snow and mud are the easiest surfaces on which to see tracks, although with

Black bear track

practice, or what master tracker Tom Brown Jr. calls "dirt time," you will begin to notice tracks and trails in other types of terrain. Each track tells a story, of an animal and its life and sometimes its death.

Signs that animals leave can be the scrapes on a tree from a buck's antlers or a bear's claws, the nibbled ends of grasses made by a rabbit or other foraging critter, or the holes hollowed out of a tree trunk by a woodpecker. Signs could also be hickory or walnut shells chewed open and left on an old stone, piles of pine cone litter left by a squirrel, or the turkey carcass and feathers and bones left by a pack of coyotes. The signs left by the more-than-human world are varied and diverse. They can help us open our minds, hearts, and senses. We can become aware of the life and death struggles as well as the beauty all around us and within the folds of the living earth.

Scat is the fecal matter animals leave behind. Each animal's scat is unique, and each species' scat has certain characteristics that can be helpful in identifying that animal. Bear scat tends to be large and is deposited in a pile, often with lots of seeds visible, whereas deer scat looks like pellets anywhere from a quarter to a half inch in length, although this can vary. Foxes and coyotes tend to leave more elongated stools, often with fur and small bones visible, depending on the prey the animal last ate.

This book isn't intended to be a comprehensive guide to tracking, as there are many great field guides you can get to help you identify the animals in your area. What I would like to offer you here is a way to begin thinking about the tracks you encounter on your morning or afternoon walks or out on the land for your nature meditation. Like all of the skills you are learning as you rewild your life, tracking is one that improves over time, with one type of track laying the foundation for identifying others. For instance, you might begin by learning to identify the hoof prints of the white-tailed deer or the hopping pattern of the common but very cool grey squirrel. Once you know one basic track, you can begin to learn about the varied tracks that animal makes when its gait or speed of movement changes. You'll also learn the straddle (the distance from left to right between the tracks) and the stride (the length between individual tracks). Each of these measurements can be helpful in identifying the kind of animal you are tracking, and they also tell you something about what the animal was doing at the time he made the tracks.

You may begin to notice that an animal you are tracking has a recurring daily pattern of movement. Animals tend to be creatures of habit, moving along the same paths on a regular basis, often creating paths, or runs, you can become familiar with. Once you recognize these patterns, you also have a responsibility to cause as little disturbance as possible to the animal or animals. If you know the daily patterns of a small herd of white-tailed deer, for instance, you can sit in a place close enough to observe them but stay far enough away so that your presence does not alarm them.

One of the great rewards of tracking is becoming familiar with both a single animal you share the land with and the various other species. Birds leave tracks, signs, and scat, and because they are easy to observe during the day, they can be a wonderful creature to begin to track. In the springtime, when backyard birds are nesting, you may get to know a single bird or a family of birds. Because a single nesting family stays in one location, you can get to know the individual birds as well as characteristics of that species. The same is true for squirrels, rabbits, and other common backyard animals. They are not as elusive as the nocturnal creatures we often know are present only by the tracks they leave behind. I love keeping tabs on the family of chipmunks living under our front stairs.

When you get to know individual animals who live near you, you also will become familiar with the daily cycle of predator and prey. Even though it can be shocking or sad to lose one of these animals you enjoyed observing, it does help you gain a greater understanding and connection with the living earth.

Animal trails—or runs, as I mentioned earlier—reveal the regular patterns of movement of a certain animal or species. These trails often look like subtle pathways through tall grasses or tunnels underneath thick-growing bushes. They can also look like a trail running through the land, with multiple tracks layered on top of one another.

To more easily find the runs left by animals, it can be helpful to get down low and see the landscape the way the creature you are tracking would see it. Animals see the world from a much different perspective than we do. Getting down on all fours can help you begin to see through their eyes and perhaps even begin to anticipate where they might be heading and why. While you are down there, you can also look for any signs of browsing—such as grasses or other plants that have been chewed, nibbled, pulled up, or otherwise eaten. You may also see smaller trails, runs, or tunnels down on the ground or under the snow, which would be left by mice, voles, or other small rodents that feed larger predators. Perhaps you will also see ants, worms, and other tiny, tiny creatures moving through the avenues, trails, and runs beneath the grass. There are truly worlds inside of worlds all the way down.

ANIMAL-TRACK MANDALA MEDITATION

When you find an animal's tracks, get down low on the land so you can look at it closely. Kneel, squat, or lie down on your belly. Get close enough so that you can see all of the features of the track—the depressions from the individual toe pads or claws, the punches in the soil from the nails, and any variations in the depth of the tracks.

Whether or not you can identify the animal who made this track, take time to study the track intently, as if it were a mandala designed to deepen meditation. As you gaze at the track, let go of whatever else you might be doing. Let your attention be single pointed, as you scan all of the small features. Smell the earth and the air around you, and notice

if you can pick up any scents left behind by the
creature. Some animals, like fox, leave a musky scent.
Imagine the animal stepping on this exact piece of
earth before you were here. Open your awareness to
the presence of this animal, feel the animal here in
this space with you, and allow your awareness to rise
up to the sky, as if you were a hawk soaring. Stretch
your mind with this awareness and sense where this
animal might be at this moment.

Then take a few breaths and feel how the earth
underneath you and the air all around you is like an
ocean that connects you with the spirit and presence
of this wild being. Take a moment to express
gratitude for the gift of this track and respect for the
thread that connects you with this creature.

Make time to be completely present with each track. This skill takes
time to improve. Try not to get frustrated if you find it hard to find
tracks or if they are difficult to identify. In hunter-gatherer cultures,
these skills were learned from early childhood. You wouldn't expect to
be fluent in a foreign language after learning a few words. Keep a field
guide for animal tracks with you and keep learning.

Rewilding offers many pathways for connecting with the miraculous life-forms on this good earth, from walking with awareness and
sharpening our senses, to becoming intimate with our land and harvesting sustenance from it. Through mindfulness, we come to the
living earth as ourselves, as we are in this moment. We come back
into relationship with the earth through a renewed relationship with
ourselves as sentient, sensitive, and highly adaptable.

We sit in meditative awareness, receiving breath and offering our
life presence to evolution's unfolding. What happens when our tailbone rests directly on the earth and we take in the smell of dried
white-pine branches crackling and popping in our small fire? What
happens when we sit in stillness and reverence and watch the afternoon slip into evening? Who are we who bring this consciousness to

the earth? Could it be that we ourselves are the planet, that we are biped planetary neurons giving the living earth the opportunity to experience itself through our complex nervous systems? We hold the great pendulum of our own possibility, the possibility of a peaceful and harmonious presence on this planet. When we connect with the living earth, we are no longer at war with the life systems that support us; instead, we become their dedicated caretakers. When we bring our present-moment awareness into the woods and fields and reintroduce ourselves to the more-than-human world we have been missing for so long, life as we know it will change.

Knowing that you love the Earth changes you,
activates you to defend and protect and celebrate.
But when you feel that the Earth loves you in
return, that feeling transforms the relationship
into a sacred bond.

ROBIN WALL KIMMERER

6

PUTTING IT ALL TOGETHER

A Rewilding Flow

Rewilding is an ongoing journey. The exploration, learning, and discovery never end. It has been a relatively short time since our bond with nature and her living beings has been lost. It is up to each of us to reconnect and to rediscover our wild nature.

My Italian ancestors were hunters, gardeners, mushroom foragers, and wine and pasta makers. They loved their food and their wine. They knew their land, and they harvested great joy from its simple and delicious pleasures. Whatever region on whichever continent your ancestors lived, they held extensive knowledge of its ways. Somewhere in your family's past, probably not too many generations ago, your relatives loved their land, or at least knew it well. When I walk in the spring woods looking for morel mushrooms, I feel a connection with my fungus-loving ancestors.

Walk anywhere outdoors and notice the different plants, weeds, stones, insects, clouds, and birds. How many can you name? Which plants and weeds do you know how to use for food or medicine? Can you look at the sky and tell what type of weather is on the way? Do you know what kind of wood makes the best fire?

Our ancestors knew a lot more about these things than we do today. We have gained many conveniences from our modern way of life, but we have also lost many vital connections along the way. The practice of rewilding does not have to mean discarding the good in our modern life, but it does mean stepping out to actively reclaim some of the good we have lost. Perhaps in remembering just a little of what our ancestors once knew, we can bring something important to our lives and our world today.

Creating fire with a bow drill is a skill that may seem beyond reach, until you finally do it. I didn't think I could do it, until I did. I also didn't think that I could learn how to fashion arrowheads out of flint, but with a little practice I learned how. And it was so much fun and so rewarding. You want to begin with whatever you find interesting or fun. What do you love the most about nature and being outside? Is it walking, running, hiking? Doing yoga outdoors? Perhaps you love to meditate on the sound of the wind or walk barefoot on the earth. Maybe you love to fish or to forage. Perhaps you love finding and following animal tracks or watching birds. Any of these are perfect entry points for a rewilding journey.

Practice being comfortable with what you don't know. You are not in a contest to see who can identify the most plants or who can weave the neatest basket. If anything, rewilding will help you stress less. You may find that even when driving down the road in your car, you can now better see the contours of the earth's body in the hills and valleys, that you can feel the breath of life on your skin and in your lungs, that you can feel the kiss of starlight in the noonday sun, and that you can feel gratitude for the gift of this precious moment.

Becoming intimate with place and really knowing, loving, and being in relationship with the earth grows slowly over time. Like any relationship, it deepens through experience and is nurtured with consistency and care. As the seasons turn, one by one, bringing us home again to the smell of fall and the joy of spring, our memories of years gone by are stirred. We are traveling through outer space on this living orb, sharing our breath, our water, and our bodies with other life-forms throughout time. Wherever you live, I invite you to get to know your trees, your stones, your animal neighbors. As you get to know your land, the stones, sticks, plants, and creatures will become your friends and keep you company. How can we ever be alone on this earth among the variety of such beautiful beings?

> No two robins are ever the same. . . . Each is as different as you and I, and we can never exhaust the possibilities of learning something new each time we observe a robin. This is also true of everything else in life, every experience, every situation, every bird, tree, rock, water, and leaf, for we can never know enough about anything. Finally, you do not even begin to know an animal until you touch it and feel its spirit. Then and only then can you ever begin to know.   STALKING WOLF[1]

Integrating Your Skills

In this chapter, we will take all of the concepts, practices, meditations, and skills we've covered and combine them into a sequence you can use to support your practice of rewilding. This sequence contains ten steps, each of which you could concentrate on for a lifetime. You can explore alone or with others on a rewilding quest. Your solitary wanderings and musings should be shared with others who can appreciate your love of the land and who care about it, too.

I also encourage you to take a break from social media when you are outdoors. Resist the urge to capture the moments with a photo on your phone. See if you can enjoy something special and private and not share it with the world. How is the experience different when it is not connected to an experience of being validated, judged, or simply known by a larger social network?

Solitude, Loneliness, and Safety

We all spend time outdoors either alone or with people. *Thank you, Captain Obvious!* My point is that there are different ways of being alone and different ways of being with people. I have spent a lot of time alone in the woods, and I enjoy it. I find it peaceful and rejuvenating. I like being alone with my thoughts while immersed in the more-than-human world. I can let my ego go. I don't have to be anyone. I can just be. When we are alone, no one is watching us, analyzing us, judging us. Instead, the more-than-human world is your witness.

Who are you outside the boundaries of your social network? What can you let go of, and what can you be with, when you give yourself the gift of time alone in nature? Even an hour alone, unplugged, to practice the essential art of presence can do wonders for the heart, refreshing mind and spirit.

Sometimes while spending solo time in nature, I admit I have felt lonely and wished I had someone to share it with. And sometimes I have even felt scared. As with yoga, meditation, and other contemplative practices, there is an aloneness to rewilding. But there is a difference between being alone and being lonely. If you can learn to be alone outdoors, alone as it relates to the human world, yet be open and connected to the more-than-human world, you will be alone without being lonely. The trees and stones themselves will reach out to you in their own ways, speak to you in their own languages, and share with you what they have to give.

With that understanding, it is also true that knowing you have community to return to, people who are interested in hearing your story, people you can share your harvest with, people who have seen you grow, this is a treasure indeed. And it is possible to find other people who enjoy being outdoors in mindful awareness together. One of my favorite things about training outdoor guides and leading rewilding retreats is when a group of thirty or more modern humans walk through a forest in great awareness and relative silence. After thirty minutes of moving mindfully through the woods as a group, many are often amazed that such a thing was possible. There is a connection that happens, one that goes beyond verbal language, when we spend this kind of time together outside. There are old ways of being together in deep awareness, where the skills of listening and speaking from the heart are developed to a high art form. This is a technique in rewilding that our time is in sore need of, one that nourishes more than the body.

We will explore the art of sharing in community as part of the rewilding journey in the final step of our rewilding flow.

There are some real dangers outdoors, so whether you are alone or with other human beings, it is important to be aware of your surroundings. People often fear wildlife such as bears, snakes, and mountain lions, but unfortunately, we are more likely to be in danger from members of our own species than from an animal relative. Fear of nature is epidemic in our culture today; ticks, mosquitoes, and other worries keep many people indoors. Part of what rewilding is about is putting those fears into proper perspective. We must acknowledge the reality that there are people out there who can be dangerous and that bad things can happen outdoors. So, be aware of your surroundings. Use mindfulness to increase your awareness in a situation. Trust your instincts. If a place, a person, or a situation doesn't feel right, listen to your gut and keep yourself safe. If you plan on spending time alone outdoors, you will need to rely on yourself, your skills, and your know-how. Choose places you are comfortable in, bring what you need, and always let someone know where you are and when you will be back.

If you fear being alone outdoors, don't let it stop you. Find a friend to go with you or a like-minded group. You can agree to spend time in silence together, walking with awareness and enjoying the land without the need for talking. After a time of walking in silence, you can agree to talk about what each of you has noticed. After you've visited a place a few times with company, try going alone if it feels safe. Over time, as your comfort grows, you can gradually expand your boundaries, perhaps even getting to the point where you can sleep outside one night all by yourself!

Mindful Rewilding Flow

The following ten steps are an effective method for feeling more calm, connected, and confident outdoors. I designed each step to address certain qualities of awareness and skills that would lead to both meditative and highly practical experiences. You may try them in order or mix and match them as you see fit. With time and practice, they can form a seamless sequence, one leading into another, much like breathing, warm-ups, postures, and relaxation form the flow in a yoga class. In fact, this mindful rewilding flow is designed to expand your mindfulness practice into new territory, allowing the forests, mountains, waterways, and other expressions of the living earth to become integral parts of your awareness. This is similar to the way that the landmarks in our body become the objects of our focus on the mat. As you become more intimate with the earth that holds you, the stones that lie steady around you, the trees that keep you company, and the many other living things moving about, they can become as much a part of you as your own breath, heart, and mind. They are, after all, made of the same stuff as we are.

Remember always to check the weather ahead of time, to tell someone where you are going and when you plan on being back, and to take your go-bag with you! Here are the ten steps we will explore in more detail in the pages ahead:

1. Intimacy with place

2. Centering

3. Breath

4. Gratitude

5. Embodiment

6. Walking with awareness

7. Engaging and expanding all the senses

8. Nature meditation and observation

9. Bushcraft

10. Share circle

Step 1: Intimacy with Place

> The mountain says you live in a particular place. Though
> it's a small area, just a square mile or two, it took me
> many trips to even start to learn its secrets. Here there
> are blueberries, and here there are bigger blueberries.
> You pass a hundred different plants along the trail;
> I know maybe twenty of them. One could spend a
> lifetime learning a small range of mountains, and once
> upon a time people did.   **BILL MCKIBBEN**

The first step in this process is to become curious about the land you live with. You may already have knowledge of the ecosystems around you or the history of people on your land, but seek to expand that as you replace information with true connection. Learning about the history of the land you live on adds depth and richness to your time outdoors. It can also help you to become an engaged and active ambassador for the more-than-human world. Take some time prior to heading out to learn about the place you are exploring.

Even before diving into the geological history of a place, I often try to learn the indigenous history. In North America, the indigenous cultures were, and are, affected dramatically, displaced and traumatized by colonization. Disease, genocide, and the forcible relocation of First Nation peoples continue to affect their descendants today. It is important to acknowledge this past and to consider how it affects our present. Who are the First Nation peoples that call this land home? What is their history as they tell it? Often the story of indigenous cultures is told by the culture that conquered them. Seek out the original people's history so that their voice may be heard and acknowledged. Many First Nation communities continue today. The magnitude of unsought changes colonization forced upon indigenous peoples compels us to become aware of the true history and how it affects lives today. I believe that this is a critical part of any process of drawing closer to the earth and helping to heal the wounds of the past.

It is also powerful to learn about the geological history of your land. What kinds of rocks and minerals are under your feet? How do they affect the soil underneath? What grows on the land based on the soil composition? What animals live there, and what are their habits? What kinds of plants and trees are native to the area? What types of invasive plants are here and how are they affecting the delicate balance of the ecosystem? How has the land been shaped by human civilization? How has it been shaped by geological processes and climate changes such as glaciers, floods, and other large-scale phenomena? What kind of weather is common now and what has it been like in the past? What is the recent human history of this land? The more we learn about our land, the more connected we feel to it and the greater our understanding of its character and story.

Organizations like the Audubon Society and other conservation groups local to your area have a great deal of knowledge about the land, plants, and animals. They maintain preserves and conservation lands that are usually easy to frequent and become familiar with. If there are tribal lands and organizations near you, seek them out to learn what history they share with the public. State and federal parks also offer tremendous educational opportunities for those curious to learn the history of a local environment. Town historical societies can also be valuable resources on local history. Each town and village have their own unique story. You might be surprised by the fascinating tales that happened in your own area.

This first step is one that truly never ends and could easily fill up the time each of us has on earth. As we recognize our part in the history of our land, perhaps the gifts we give through our own passion for nature's gifts will go on, as we become part of the history for those who are yet to come.

Step 2: Centering

> I only went out for a walk, and finally concluded
> to stay out till sundown, for going out, I found,
> was really going in.   JOHN MUIR

Centering is when you invite your attention into the present moment, which is when you have the power of skillful action. Getting centered in the present, coming home to your body and breath, is where mindfulness begins. Often, when we practice mindfulness, we notice how our minds tend to wander from one thought to another. This is natural and not something to judge or to get frustrated about—just practice noticing the wandering and gently bring your attention back to the moment.

Take a few moments to center yourself before you head out on the land. It makes all the difference in the world. Outdoor educator and bird language expert John Young describes it best as inviting your awareness to become greater than your disturbance. I have found that by centering myself at the beginning of a mindful outdoor experience, my mind becomes more still, my senses sharper, and my awareness more expansive. I notice things I might miss otherwise, such as the sounds of the birds or wind in the trees, and my own impact on the environment is lessened as I walk with greater care and attention.

One mild late-spring afternoon in my late twenties, I was walking through the woods behind my father's house in Connecticut, on the trail from the old Bear Cave. Placing my feet carefully on stones or softened places in the trail, I concentrated on creating as little sound or disturbance as possible. As I watched my steps, a small garter snake in a patch of sunlight in the middle of the trail came into view. It was curled up and seemed to be sleeping. I paused to absorb the beauty and presence of this little snake. I then scanned the ground to my left and right and was surprised to see a fawn, white spots and all, curled up fast asleep about three feet off the trail. Had I fox walked into an animal day care? I stood quietly for a moment and then tip-toed around the snake to keep going. Neither the snake nor the fawn seemed to notice I had even passed.

Practicing mindful rewilding is different from more common meditation practices because you are in the presence of the living earth and the more-than-human world. Unlike classical forms of meditation, where the mind is held to a single point of focus such as a candle flame or the breath, rewilding allows you to let your awareness scan the environment. Because the outdoors is such a rich, dynamic space, it contains many things to explore and be fascinated by. So the practice is to become aware when your attention has wandered into stories in your own mind. When you first head outside, you may find that your mind is preoccupied by your inner dialogue. When this happens, take a deep breath in, let it out with a gentle sigh, and come back to the presence of the earth. Keep doing this, and in time you'll find your awareness has expanded. All the other ingredients hinge on this core practice.

One night, while in residency at Goddard College, I decided to take a walk in the woods after dinner. It was February and cold. The sun had just set, but there was still a faint light in the west. I stood on the edge of the woods and centered myself. I closed my eyes and inhaled and then exhaled deeply a couple of times, keeping the lungs empty for several seconds. When I felt a strong urge to inhale, I took a deep breath in while simultaneously feeling the life force climbing up my spine, all the way to the crown of my head. When I let the breath out, I just felt the effect. This yogic practice often makes me feel a surge of energy and a sense that my awareness is expanding, and when I open my eyes, everything is more vivid and clear.

On this evening, as I held my breath after exhaling, I allowed my awareness to venture into the space before me. I felt the quality of the woods and myself opening to the land. After inhaling, I held that sense of expanding awareness and an intent to remain sensitive to the land. Then I took a few careful steps into the forest, when I suddenly heard the sound of another being's loud exhalation—large lungs emptying out through big nostrils. My adrenaline surged when I sensed a male white-tailed deer just ahead. It bounded away, but its presence stayed with me. I continued on into the dark woods for a beautiful night walk, knowing I was in a space where I was not the master, knowing I needed to walk with respect and presence.

When we meditate on our cushion indoors, we confront the fears that live within us, the contents of our minds and bodies. Out in the field, immersed in the web of life, we encounter fears and challenges outside us, and we receive gifts and lessons in relationship with our extended self—the living, breathing, very dynamic universe. Both paths are important and complementary.

Guided Centering

When you arrive at the beginning of your rewilding location, take a few moments to stand still, drawing your attention inward. Close your eyes, or soften your gaze. Take a deep breath in and let it out with a sigh. Let go of your day and arrive in your body in this moment. Allow your awareness to move out of the thinking mind and into the feeling body. If you were describing the weather conditions inside yourself right now, what would they be? Dark and stormy? Sunny and warm? Foggy? Clear? Simply notice. For the duration of your time in the forest, let yourself set aside your to-do list, your worries, and your plans. Give yourself permission to simply be. As we like to say in Kripalu Yoga, "Nothing to do, nowhere to go, at home in the body." Allow yourself this time to wander and to enjoy the beauty of the earth.

Step 3: Breath

Breathing in, I calm body and mind. Breathing out, I smile. Dwelling in the present moment I know this is the only moment.   THICH NHAT HANH

The third foundational practice of mindful rewilding is slowing and deepening the breath. The first thing anyone does when they come into this world is take a breath. The last thing anyone does before they leave this life is let go with the final breath. Throughout our life journey, breath anchors us in the present moment; it is our most vital connection to life. We can go over twenty days without food, and two to three days without water, but we can only survive two to three minutes without breathing. As noted earlier, the atmosphere we breathe has been recycled here on our planet for a few billion years. We breathe in the oxygen that the trees and oceans exhale, while they breathe in the carbon dioxide that we exhale. This dance of reciprocity and interbeing is the matrix of life we are woven into.

Slow, deep breathing has a calming effect on the nervous system that allows us to shift from the fight-or-flight response to the relaxation response. This is incredibly important because in fight-or-flight, we are reactive—we act without thinking about the consequences. This reaction is critical when we are in a life-or-death situation, but otherwise, reactivity can cause more harm than good. Consider a time when you reacted to someone or something in anger or fear and reflect on the outcome. More often than not, reactions cause suffering.

The ability to remain calm and think clearly in stressful situations is a must. Most outdoor survival experts will tell you that this single ability is the primary determinant of surviving a life-threatening emergency in the wild. Learning to slow and deepen the breath is a critical skill in mindful rewilding, not only for expanding awareness but also for keeping cool and acting with skill.

Here is a simple and effective technique for slow deep breathing:

- Draw a deep breath in through your nose.

- As you exhale through your mouth, let the exhalation be at least twice as long as the inhalation.

- Repeat three to ten times.

- Notice how you feel.

Guided Breath

Before you begin to move into the woods or over the land, close your eyes and breathe a deep breath in through the nose, letting it out slowly through the mouth. Repeat this simple breath for three to ten cycles, focusing on the sensation of the breath flowing in and out. Let go of thoughts, tension, and worries. Feel your feet planted on the solid earth and the crown of your head reaching up toward the sky. Notice the environment inside of you. Notice your thoughts. Your inner state is the presence you bring onto the land. Your presence sends out ripples of energy. Keep breathing, in and out, until you begin to feel spacious, calm, and clear. Begin to sense the living earth all around you. Feel the air moving, listen to the sounds of nature, and smell the atmosphere. When you are ready, allow your eyes to open and notice what you see and sense. As you begin your trek in nature, stay with your breath and feel the earth through your breathing.

Step 4: Gratitude

We are thankful to our Mother the Earth, for she gives us everything that we need for life. She supports our feet as we walk about upon her. It gives us joy that she still continues to care for us, just as she has from the beginning of time. To our Mother, we send thanksgiving, love, respect. Now our minds are one.   HAUDENOSAUNEE CONFEDERACY, *Thanksgiving Address*

For many of the First Nation peoples of North America, the practice of gratitude is foundational to their way of life. Perhaps the most famous example comes from the Haudenosaunee Confederacy, known more commonly as the Iroquois, the name given them by the French. Taking time each day to reflect on the many elements of life on earth—the sun, earth, water, plants, herbs, animals, and the life-giving winds—is a core practice of the Haudenosaunee culture. Of course, the Thanksgiving holiday celebrated on the fourth Thursday in November each year in the United States was inspired and modeled by the Wampanoag People in what is today Massachusetts.

Take a moment to bring your attention to something you feel thankful for. It could be your breath, a loved one, a kind gesture someone showed you. Notice how reflecting on this affects your inner state. When you immerse yourself in the earth's embrace, give yourself permission to stop and be with anything that feels like a gift. Anything at all can be an opportunity to strengthen the gratitude muscle. This practice becomes easier the more you do it.

Another important thing to remember when moving over the earth is that you are entering a home. Other beings dwell here and know every branch and stone. Feel the reality that you are a guest here. Be respectful and courteous. Notice how this shift in attitude and embrace of gratitude changes your experience in the woods.

GRATITUDE

Before moving into nature, take a moment to
acknowledge that you are a guest in this place and
that other beings call this land home. Close your eyes
or soften your gaze. Feel the atmosphere around
you, the quality of the temperature. Sense the earth

below your feet and the Standing People beside
you, the trees. Listen for our winged friends talking
in the forest. Feel the pulse and dance of the life of
which you are a part. Breathe and extend gratitude
for all that life is offering up to you in this moment.
Invite a sense of contentment, of having enough.
Take a breath into this affirmation: I am content
and grateful.

Step 5: Embodiment

In the Katha Upanishad, one of the ancient texts of yoga, it is taught
that the body is a chariot we ride through life. The idea is that
our spirit inhabits this body as a vehicle, experiencing the wonders
of earth through the senses. In this context, yoga is a discipline
to support the body in becoming the most finely tuned and effective vehicle in which to experience what it is to be a human being
and achieve our greatest potential. Considering all of the wonders
that surround us outdoors and the varied terrain we are gifted with
navigating on the land, knowing our body's capabilities supports
mindful movement and mindful experience as we explore the earth
with awareness.

For this reason, the fifth step in this process is what I call embodiment. It includes some gentle warm-ups and stretches to help you
connect with the body, lubricate the joints, and support a greater integration of body, breath, and mind. This integration of our primary
functions is the foundation of yoga and can enhance your experience
of rewilding exponentially. That said, do not be limited by what is
outlined in these pages. You may have embodiment practices such as
yoga, tai chi, qi gong, or another movement discipline that supports a
strong, flexible, integrated, and sensitive body. Any of these will prepare you for your time outdoors.

WARM-UP 1: JOINT ROTATIONS

This series is effective for lubricating the major joint areas in the body, as well as for stretching, strengthening, and toning the major muscle groups, so that your movement on the land can be graceful, fluid, and stable. Stay conscious of your breathing as you move through these movements.

1. **Ankle Rotations.** From a standing position, step one foot behind you so that the top of the foot is on the ground and the heel is pointing to the sky. Begin to make circles with the heel, rotating the ankle joint. After ten rounds, move in the other direction. After you have completed one side, extend the other foot out behind you and repeat. When you are done, step the feet together, close your eyes, and take two to four deep breaths. Notice how you feel.

2. **Knee Rotations.** Step your feet together, bend your knees, lengthen your torso, and place your hands on top of the knees so that the inner knees are touching. Begin to make small circles with the knees, allowing the ankles to flex as you go around in one direction for five to fifteen cycles. When you are ready, reverse the direction of the movement. Come to standing when you are done, close your eyes, and take two to four deep breaths. Notice how you feel.

3. **Hip Circles.** Step your feet a little wider than hip distance apart. Place your hands on your hips and begin to make circles with your hips. You might imagine that you are using your hips to clean out the inside of a peanut butter jar! Allow the circles to grow gradually wider and wider until you decide it is time to reverse the direction. When you feel balanced and complete, step the feet together, stand up tall, take two to four deep breaths, and notice how you feel in your body.

4. **Spinal Flexion and Extension.** Let your feet be hip distance apart. Bend your knees and place your hands just above the knees. As you inhale, extend your chest forward and lift the chin, gently stretching the front line of the torso. As you exhale, tuck the chin toward the sternum and arch the spine like a scared Halloween cat. Continue to move with the breath, inhaling the heart forward and exhaling as you tuck the chin and arch the spine. Continue for five to ten breaths and then come to standing. Take two to four deep, integrating breaths. Notice how you feel.

5. **Spinal Twists.** Stand with your feet a little wider than hip distance apart. Let your arms hang by your sides like empty coat sleeves. Begin to gently twist from side to side, allowing your arms to swing and thump against your torso on each side. Allow your head and neck to turn as you swing from side to side. If you would like, try integrating your breath into the movement by inhaling to center and exhaling to each side. Continue for one to two minutes and then come to center and take a few deep breaths. Notice how you feel.

6. **Shoulder Rolls.** Standing upright, roll the shoulders up toward your ears and forward, then down and back, in undulating circles. Let the arms hang by your sides. When you are ready, reverse the direction. Before you finish, take a deep breath in and pull the shoulders up to your ears. Hold in the breath. Scrunch up your face really, really tight, like you just bit into a lemon. Make fists with your hands. Keep holding and then exhale and let the tension go with a sigh. Notice how you feel.

7. **Wrist Openers.** Inhale and stretch your arms out to the side at shoulder height. Now reach them straight out in front of you, thumbs up, and interlace your fingers. Bend the elbows at ninety degrees and begin to make circles with your wrists. After about thirty seconds reverse the direction. When you feel complete, allow your arms to hang by your sides and take a few deep breaths. Notice how you feel.

8. **Neck Rotations.** Standing tall and looking straight ahead, begin to make small circles with your nose. Allow the circles to get larger and larger, staying connected to your breathing as you go around. When you are ready, reverse the direction. When you feel complete, return your chin to level, looking ahead. Take a few deep breaths and notice how you feel.

As you begin to move and walk, try to stay aware of your body in space, as well as the many ways that your senses interact with the environment.

Warm-Up 2: Mindful Push-Ups

1. Come into Plank position, with your arms straight and your hands below your shoulders, as if you're going to do a push-up, with your toes curled under and your heels pressing out into space behind you. Position your hips so that they are suspended directly between your heels and shoulders. Firm up the abdominal wall and lengthen out the spine through the crown of your head. Find your breath and allow it to slowly deepen.

2. On an exhalation, bend the elbows slightly, lowering your nose toward the earth. Come as far down as you can safely. On an inhalation, press back up to Plank. Repeat the movement in harmony with your breath until you feel too tired to continue.

3. Inhale and let your legs and tops of the feet lower to the ground. Then arch your torso gently into Upward-Facing Dog position, with your shoulders back and down. Press firmly into the earth with the hands and the tops of the feet, taking care to avoid any excessive arching in the low back.

4. As you exhale, lift your hips up and back until your head comes between your arms into Downward-Facing Dog. Feel the shoulders slide away from your ears and press the palms firmly into the earth. Feel free to alternately bend the knees, stretching out the back of each leg as you exhale. Allow your spine to be long, and don't worry if your heels don't touch the floor—it isn't the point of the pose.

5. Repeat moving between Upward- and Downward-Facing Dog, letting the breath guide the movement. Inhale into Upward-Facing Dog, and exhale into Downward-Facing Dog.

6. From Downward-Facing Dog, step the feet toward the hands coming into Standing-Forward Fold. Clasp alternate elbows and hang here for a few breaths.

7. Slide the hands to the hips, bend the knees, lengthen the torso, and hinge up to standing.

8. Take two to four deep breaths and notice how you feel.

WARM-UP 3: SUN BREATHS

1. Stand with your feet hip distance apart.

2. As you inhale, lift your arms up overhead until your palms come together at the very peak of the inhalation.

3. As you exhale, slowly lower your arms so that they come to rest by your sides at the very bottom of the exhalation.

4. Continue for one to two minutes, focusing your attention on your breathing and the sensations you notice as you move. Do your best to make the movement of the arms mirror your deepest and most

complete breath. This may mean slowing down a
lot and letting the sensation become a bit stronger.

5. When you are complete, take two to four
    integrating breaths and notice how you feel.

When you have completed your embodiment
practice, endeavor to bring the quality of attention that
you now carry with you into your movement upon the
land. Be aware of your own presence, quality of breath,
and attention. Set an intention that your presence will
be light upon the earth, and let your movement be
relaxed, light-hearted, and curious.

Step 6: Walking with Awareness

People usually consider walking on water or in thin air
a miracle. But I think the real miracle is not to walk
either on water or in thin air, but to walk on earth.
Every day we are engaged in a miracle which we don't
even recognize: a blue sky, white clouds, green leaves,
the black, curious eyes of a child—our own two eyes.
All is a miracle.   **THICH NHAT HANH**

To consciously walk upon the earth is a simple and profound act. The
Buddha often taught that the art of mindfulness is not only to do
what you are doing but also to know that you are doing it. To truly
walk on the earth and to know the miracle of each step is no ordinary
kind of walking. It transforms one's experience of being alive. Bringing
mindful awareness to our walking allows us to combine movement
and meditation into a single action. As Thich Nhat Hanh teaches us,
walking with awareness opens us up to the moment and the profound
mystery of life. If we can be fully present for each step, and let go of
the mental filters that cloud our perception, we can experience heaven
on earth. We can shift our attention away from the work of surviving

so that we do not miss the indescribable beauty unfolding outside our homes and offices every day—the way clouds move across the blue sky, the way wind moves the trees in the afternoon light. When we put aside our worries and our responsibilities, just for a little while, we give ourselves the medicine that the living earth offers up each moment. Walking with awareness is one way to open the door to another world, one full of beauty, wonder, and depth of feeling.

Walking with awareness is an invitation to let go of our usual outcome-oriented approach to life. Work and adult responsibilities demand results. We need to know what we are doing and where we are going. Not so with this practice. In fact, I invite you to practice walking just for the sake of walking, not because you are trying to get anywhere. You may have a waterfall or a community of trees you are heading for, but I invite you to let your rewilding time be about being present and allowing your curiosity and senses to guide you. You don't have to know where the walk will lead—and for many people that is a revolutionary concept. Try to let go of your destination and enjoy the journey.

Like yoga and seated meditation, walking with awareness is much more potent when practiced along with conscious breathing. Remind yourself to be mindful of your breath, and when you notice that your mind has wandered, come back to the breath. The breath is the anchor of the mind.

Letting the Land Guide Us

> I don't like either the word or the thing. People ought to saunter in the mountains—not hike! Do you know the origin of that word "saunter"? It's a beautiful word. Away back in the Middle Ages people used to go on pilgrimages to the Holy Land, and when people in the villages through which they passed asked where they were going, they would reply, "A la sainte terre, to the Holy Land." And so they became known as sainte-terre-ers, or saunterers. Now these mountains are our Holy Land, and we ought to saunter through them reverently, not "hike" through them. JOHN MUIR

As our friend John Muir is fond of saying, hiking is a kind of walking in nature that sometimes misses the majesty of the moment in exchange for a destination. Rambling or sauntering is a more open-ended way of interacting with the landscape. When we saunter, we allow ourselves to open to fascination and to be guided. When we include the practice of mindfulness and hone our awareness to inhabit the present through our senses, we can more easily receive the landscape's way of communicating with us. When we learn to walk in this way, it can change the way we move through the world in general. We may, for instance, as we are sauntering across a field, see a lone tree and feel called to go and sit under it. This could later translate to a similar feeling while exploring career opportunities. Through our sauntering practice, we cultivate the habit of listening when something calls, even if on first glance it doesn't make sense.

J. R. R. Tolkien's writing contains many references to the power of walking. He often referred to "the road" as something like a conveyor belt. Once you step onto it, it can sweep you away. Being in nature without an agenda or a destination is another form of mindfulness meditation and can allow our brains to rest from the directed attention that modern life often requires. This practice can be a beneficial balance to the outcome-driven ways in which most people move through their days. Adjusting to this way of being is a gradual process. It can feel like moving from a fast pace to a more natural gait. Working with slow, deep breaths will help you slow down and feel your surroundings through your senses. This kind of walking can also be full of unexpected surprises, as you encounter things along the trail that delight or fascinate. A stunning sunset, a gnarled stump, or a little frog, all kinds of unexpected and delightful surprises have something to share or teach.

The Fox Walk

The Fox Walk is an awareness practice to help you walk with more attention and sensitivity that I learned from Tom Brown Jr. at the Tracker School. The goal is to walk slowly and mindfully, feeling the earth with your feet while paying attention to what is happening around you and staying connected to your breathing. You may have to unlearn what you have learned about walking throughout your life to master this skill!

Most of us walk heel-toe, which means that when we step, our heel lands first and then we roll onto the front of the foot. This way of walking came about when we started wearing shoes with heels for walking in cities and on cobblestone streets, where there is less need to be gentle and skillful in our gait. When we walked barefoot, we often walked toe-heel. Depending on the terrain and what we are doing, there are a variety of different techniques for moving quietly over the land, but this technique is fundamental and one you should know. Without soled shoes, human beings explored the terrain with the front of the foot, either placing the ball of the big toe or the ball of the pinky toe first and then rolling the heel down to the earth. When you walk this way, you have more awareness of the terrain, and you can avoid applying too much downward pressure onto twigs and sticks so that you do not make a lot of noise.

The key to really getting the most out of this practice is to go much slower than you usually do. Another trick to moving more silently is to be aware of stones in your path and to step on those because they are much quieter than leaves. Bare soil and logs are also good points of contact when endeavoring to move more silently. A student in one of my trainings once said this after a period of barefoot fox walking in the forest:

> After walking barefoot through the forest for about fifteen
> minutes, it felt like my mind just shut off, and I was
> totally engrossed by the sights, sounds, smells, and textures
> of the forest. I couldn't believe that our group of seventeen
> people could all move so silently and gracefully through
> the landscape. It felt good to go slow. It made me realize
> how I tend to charge through the woods without even
> seeing or sensing all the wonder around me. I think this
> will change the way I walk in the woods forever.

Fox Walk

Begin at the edge of a wood or field and start
by closing your eyes and deepening your breath.
Listen to the sounds of the earth and feel the
way your inner landscape and the earth's outer
landscape are connected. Acknowledge that you
exist somewhere on a spectrum between your
individual human self and the rest of the universe.
Wait until you feel empty, calm, and present. Then
open your eyes and look ahead. Standing relatively
still, take in the movements happening all around
you. You want the energy you are transmitting to
be calm, steady, and light.

When you are ready, lift one foot while looking
ahead, with your arms relaxed by your sides. Slowly
and mindfully place your foot down on the earth
big-toe side first, and then roll out to the pinky toe
side. Finally, lower your heel down, being careful
not to snap any twigs. Allow the weight of your
body to settle into the front foot before slowly
lifting the other foot. Feel that you are balancing for
a few moments on the standing foot, still looking
ahead, still calm, steady and light, and still noticing
what is moving around you. Gradually, lower the
next foot down on the big-toe side, rolling out to
the pinky-toe side and then slowly lowering the heel.
Give yourself fifteen to twenty minutes to practice
this way of moving over the land. When you are
through, notice how you feel.

When you are ready, close your eyes or soften
your gaze in front of you. Take a few deep breaths
in and out. Feel your feet making contact with the
earth. Wiggle your toes and roll onto the front
of your foot and then back into your heels. Feel
these weight-bearing parts of your feet. As you
feel into your feet, gradually firm up your thighs
as your tailbone reaches toward the earth and your
shoulders draw back and down, opening your chest.
Gradually, lengthen up the spine through the crown
of your head.

If you practice the fox walk and make it a part of your time outdoors, you will find that the concentric rings of disturbance you create
lessen and your ability to awaken your senses expands.

Moving with Wind and Shadow

Bringing these awareness skills to our time outdoors expands our
consciousness. It reveals what we are missing when we aren't truly
present to what is happening on the land. When you bring the fox
walk into your rewilding time outdoors, you will start to notice new
things. Moving through the land with minimal impact, as a part of the
landscape rather than as a distracted intruder, you'll find that creating
minimal ripples requires a relaxed kind of focus and skill.

As you walk and explore, try noticing the sound and volume of
the wind. Experiment with moving when the wind blows and then
dropping into stillness when it subsides. Use the natural sound-cover
that is generated between the wind and the vegetation all around
you to help conceal the ripples of your own movement. Also, notice
where light and shadow lie, and explore moving from shadow to
shadow. When you move in this way, you and the land are participating in a kind of collective meditation practice. You are riding the
waves of sound and silence, shadow and light, with each step becoming more and more at one with the rhythms, textures, and contours
of the earth.

This way of moving over the land can't really be labeled. It is the way that creatures who are part of the food chain must move. Because human beings have extricated ourselves from the cycle of predator and prey, we have the luxury of clomping around without a care in the world, but in this arrogance and ignorance, we have lost contact with an ancestral way of knowing the earth, a way of experiencing the merging of self and land. Such experiences of nature meditation must have been foundational to the great spiritual traditions.

Consider exploring this invitation the next time you head out.

Plant Connection

Look around at the land and the plants around you. Imagine that you can sense their roots extending deep and wide into the earth. Feel the way in which the land is connected below your feet and above your head. As you breathe, feel the breath of the earth entering your lungs. As you exhale, feel the earth inhaling your breath as well. Sense the movement of branches and twigs and the murmurings of the atmosphere swirling around you. Feel yourself immersed in the community of the plant beings surrounding you.

Invite a feeling of gratitude into your heart for the earth around you. Send this feeling out around you in all directions as you walk with mindfulness. Let your focus remain with the plants. As you saunter, allow yourself to pause and connect with any trees that call to you. You may wish to place a hand on their bark and feel, or you may want to rest your forehead against a trunk. Sit at the base of a tree with your back against the trunk in a simple meditation.

Step 7: Engaging and Expanding All the Senses

> The fragrance with which one is feasted in the woods
> is, like music, derived from a thousand untraceable
> sources . . . the whole air vibrates with myriad voices
> blended that we cannot analyze. So also, we breathe
> the fragrant violets, the rosiny pine and spicy fir, the
> rich, invigorating aroma of plushy bogs in which a
> thousand herbs are soaked.   JOHN MUIR

Our earth is a multisensory environment. The ground is uneven, with roots coming up out of the earth and ancient stones and a multitude of leaves, twigs, mosses, lichen, and fungi spread across the earth. The air is filled with the aroma of essential oils from the trees, plants, spores, water vapor, and pollen. The whirring and the songs of insects and birds surround us, and we encounter a variety of temperatures and pockets of humidity as we walk. The forest is a feast for the senses. Our eyes take in all of the colors, the dappled moonlight or the sunlight falling on the forest floor, the infinite network of limbs and twigs crisscrossing in complex patterns.

Everywhere our eyes fall, there is a mystery or a miracle to ponder. Our ears take in the sounds of wind in the trees and grasses, the call of the hawk high above, the gurgle of a cool brook, the scurrying of a squirrel digging in the leaves, the sound of our own breath, or the deep stillness of winter snow. On our skin we can feel the temperature of the forest, the roughness of the white pine's bark, and the hardness of granite that rises up out of the earth.

These sights, sounds, smells, and textures connect us with the earth and also with our ancestors. When we engage our senses and receive the full embrace of the great elements—earth, air, fire, water, space, and ether—we connect with a deep, timeless part of our humanity. Once we open the door to mindfulness in nature, we truly enter another dimension of reality, and once that door is opened, we begin to tap into a very old way of being, one that has so much value for us still.

Engaging and Expanding the Senses

As you walk with awareness, continue to breathe deeply. As you breathe, notice the aroma of the air. What earthly scents are carried on the wind? Lift your nose just slightly and inhale deeply. Draw the air deep into your nostrils and will your sense of smell to become more powerful. Breathe deeply and notice what you smell. Give yourself time to reacquaint yourself with the sense of smell, which helped us survive long ago, when the land was our home.

Look around and notice what you see. Try to take in as much of the forest as you can through your sense of sight, looking up into the canopy, down on the forest floor, and around you on all sides. Notice movement. Perhaps you detect the slightest movement of a gentle stirring of wind in the leaves or the minute movements of ants on the ground. Take a few minutes to simply gaze and take in the visual feast and constant change that is the forest.

Now shift your awareness to your sense of hearing. Notice what you can hear. Birds in the trees, leaves moved by the wind, a plane high above, or the sound of cars in the distance. Perhaps you hear a squirrel is rummaging through leaves for an acorn or your own breathing or heart beating. Take a few minutes to take in the sounds of the forest that you might otherwise miss.

Now experience your sense of touch. You may wish to find a tree and feel its bark, or you may be called to squat down and place your hand on the ground to feel the qualities of earth. You may find a stone or a boulder and allow your hands to run over its surface, or you may want to place your cheek against its cool surface. If there is water nearby, you may wish to put your hands and feet in it. Maybe you would like to remove your shoes and allow your bare feet to feel the touch of Mother Earth.

You may also taste the earth. Of course, you won't want to eat anything in nature unless you are confident it is safe and not poisonous. If you have wild edibles in your area, taste the qualities of that expression of the forest. Perhaps you can find a wild lowbush blueberry or winterberry. There is so much food and medicine in the earth, and the more we know, the more we can strengthen our bond with the place we call home.

Step 8: Nature Meditation and Observation

If one day I see a small bird and recognize it, a thin thread will form between me and that bird. If I just see it but don't really recognize it, there is no thin thread. If I go out tomorrow and see and really recognize that same individual small bird again, the thread will thicken and strengthen just a little. Every time I see and recognize that bird, the thread strengthens. Eventually it will grow into a string, then a cord, and finally a rope. This is what it means to be a Bushman. We make ropes with all aspects of the creation in this way.   SAN BUSHMAN

When I lived in the Adirondacks on Lake George, my friends and I built a beautiful shelter in the woods as part of an outdoor educational program. After we completed the structure, the sun went down, and I made a fire. Everyone left for the night, but I stayed and sat there for a few hours. I became very still and sat transfixed by the flickering flames. At one point in my meditation, a red fox trotted into the light of the fire and turned to look at me as it moved through the space. We made eye contact for a brief, dreamlike moment, and then it disappeared into the gathering darkness. In that brief moment of eye contact in the firelight,

I felt a mysterious connection with that fox. One of the fox's greatest skills is camouflage. To have such a close encounter with a creature of such mystery and stealth was a great gift. Sitting quietly in nature is how we build "ropes" with creation and in so doing establish a bond with the land and our many relatives who live there.

Another practice I learned to strengthen our bond with nature from tracker Tom Brown Jr. and his student Jon Young is called "the sit spot." This is where you go for daily meditation throughout the year, your nature meditation spot (which you established as a first step in rewilding). Unlike Eastern approaches to meditation, which tend to direct attention inwardly, the sit spot practice is an eyes-open meditation. It is a powerful practice to incorporate into your rewilding.

When you make your way to your sit spot, you create some disturbance, and the creatures of the forest are alerted to your presence. But after you sit quietly for ten or fifteen minutes, the forest goes back to its normal business, and you get a glimpse into a world you become a part of—the forest. This practice supports establishing a strong bond with place and is a great way to counteract the effects of nature deficit disorder and place blindness. You might want to bring a journal so you can sketch or record your observations.

Observing the Earth

The practice of moving with awareness has helped to prepare you (mind, body, and spirit) for the practice of sitting and observing the earth with nonjudgmental, present-moment awareness. As you move over the land, stay open to any trees, stones, or places that call you. Perhaps it is the space between roots at the base of a great tree, or perhaps there is a stone you'd like to sit on or lean against. Maybe you find a little stream to sit near so that you can listen to the water. Be open to a spot that feels safe, inviting, and comfortable. Once you've been guided to such a place, settle into a comfortable seat. Do try to maintain a long spine because this will help you remain alert for your nature meditation practice. Settle in and remain still and quiet, allowing the activity of the forest to resume, as the disturbance your entrance made fades.

As you sit, slow and deepen your breathing. Give yourself at least thirty minutes here if you can. Allow yourself to take in the sights, smells, textures, and sounds. Imagine that you are one of the boulders that calls this place home. Feel yourself sinking down into the earth, steady, stable, grounded, and present. Keep your eyes open and notice any and all movement happening around you. Awaken all of your senses one at a time, and be the witness in the woods. In a breath-based meditation, we work to hold our attention on the breath and our internal environment, but here we externalize our focus; instead of observing our thoughts, we observe the qualities and characteristics of this moment expressed through the earth.

If your focus wanders into your thoughts, come back to what is happening now in the forest. In your work with a single nature meditation spot, pay close attention to the individual plants and animals that are there. Each time you return to this spot, see if you can recognize these members of the forest community. You may notice a squirrel or a chickadee who lives near your spot. Each time you can recognize that creature, your bond grows stronger, and you will feel more intimately connected with this place. When it is time to complete your sit, take a deep breath, and as you exhale, send your gratitude to this community for the opportunity to experience its gifts.

If you like, you can try the following meditation as you sit or even as you complete your sit: Breathing in I feel my body (eyes closed). Breathing out I feel the earth (eyes open). Let your exhalation be twice as long as your inhalation. Repeat for two to five minutes.

Step 9: Bushcraft

Before enlightenment, chopping wood and carrying water. After enlightenment, chopping wood and carrying water. **ZEN PROVERB**

Bushcraft refers to the vast array of skills involved in living close to the earth, using mostly what the land around you has to offer. Bushcrafting communities and groups are sometimes called *ancestral skills enthusiasts*. These terms certainly relate to the work of human rewilding. Bushcraft can include skills such as bow and hand drill, flint and steel, shelter building, tracking, foraging, toolmaking, basketmaking, pottery, woodworking, and making cordage out of natural fibers. Bushcraft encompasses the skills necessary to make one's home in the wild.

Within the context of our mindful rewilding flow, this step grounds the practice in practical skills. Sometimes in the worlds of mindfulness, yoga, and meditation, we can get caught in abstractions, high ideals, and even righteousness. Modern spiritual people suffer from nature disconnection along with the rest of society. Getting out of theory and philosophy and into the development of practical skills to attend to our basic needs brings all of the lofty ideas down to earth.

Living off the grid with my parents was an early experience with bushcraft. It wasn't until I was later introduced to the bow-drill technique of making fire that bushcrafting skills took hold of me at a deep level. The man who taught me the technique spoke about the skill with a passion and wonder and excitement that caught my attention. We spent a whole day building my first kit out of white cedar. It was not easy, and I struggled with the technique—but when I was finally gifted with my first coal and breathed life into my first tinder nest, holding fire in the palm of my hand, my life changed forever. That experience brought the ancient past and the present moment into union. I felt at one with my ancestors and my progeny to come. Being the conduit for the primal force of fire was empowering and awe-inspiring.

Over time, my passion for using a bow drill led me to the practice of archery using a primitive bow rather than a manufactured modern compound bow. A traditional "self-bow" is simply a single piece of wood with a string, a "bent stick" as we like to say. I purchased a handmade longbow and began to shoot on my days off. My yoga and meditation practice merged beautifully with archery. When my mind wandered, my shots went astray; when I became absolutely focused and present, when my awareness merged with the single point of the target, my shots found home. It was a practice of total focus and nonattachment to outcome.

As the years went by, I learned to build my own bows and arrows. I also learned how to fashion stone tools from flint and bone and more about foraging for wild foods and making shelters. Yet all of the skills I now have are but the tip of the iceberg of ancestral knowledge. Even at this elementary level, I have found such satisfaction and joy in this learning and the practices. That is what I wish for you, too.

After nature meditation practice, transitioning to a bushcraft project is a beautiful way to take your meditation into the practice of a concrete skill. Whatever you may be working on—building a debris shelter, honing your tracking skills, making fire, foraging for wild food, whittling a tool out of wood—bring your present-moment awareness and gratitude to your work. The ideal setting for bushcrafting is your own camp, somewhere outdoors where you can be alone or with friends. Having your own campsite will allow you to construct a simple shelter, make fire, establish a nature meditation location, and begin to know a place well.

Of course, not everyone is in a location where establishing a camp is possible. You may not even be in a place where you can make a proper fire. That is okay. There are some bushcraft skills you can work on in your apartment or in a small park.

Wherever you find yourself, focusing on your project and enjoying the passing of the day will connect you to the land and a way of being that our ancestors knew. There is a simplicity and a peace that comes from engaging in practical work. We can also bring an ethic of selflessness and service to our bushcrafting. I invite you to imagine that whatever you are doing is not for you but an offering of thanks to that which you hold to be most divine and sacred. Strive to make your work, your craft, a reflection of your love and gratitude for the earth and the gift of your life. Think of each and every bushcraft project as both practical and artistic, an expression of your soul's longing.

When your project has been completed, the final step in this process is gathering with others in a circle of community to share what is true and real in your heart. No human is an island, and all life is connected. We can only truly thrive in compassionate and supportive relationship with our friends and family. Council practice is a tried-and-true method for strengthening the bonds of human connection and learning to develop our communication skills. Concluding your day or your rewilding experience with a council practice allows the wisdom of the group to be shared by all, so that everyone may learn and grow in community.

Step 10: Share Circle

An important part of the rewilding process is learning how to live in relationship to circles again. The modern world is based on right angles, squares, and linearity, but nature moves in circles, spirals, whorls, vortexes, and torsion cycles. This is evident in almost everything we see in the living earth. People, too, once gathered in circles, in circular shelters, or simply around the central gathering point of the community fire, where they told stories, shared wisdom, and listened deeply. The elders spun stories of the culture's learning, while the flickering fire lulled the people into a high-band alpha brain wave, a trance state on their way to sleep and dreams. Children snuggled in close as the darkness closed in all around, and looking up, all could see the canvas of infinity with a million tiny lights flickering and the occasional shooting star.

Share your rewilding experience. Perhaps you saw a red fox going about its daily hunt or a chickadee land on a branch to hang out with you for a few moments, or perhaps you had an insight while watching the wind blow the clouds across the sky. Telling our story and listening deeply to the stories of others is a powerful medicine in itself. In a council session, it can be especially powerful.

Often in share circles it can be nice to use a "talking piece," whether a stone or some other natural object. The only person in the group who may speak is the one who is holding the piece, which is passed around the circle in a clockwise direction so that each person has an opportunity to speak. After each person shares, the group takes a deep breath in together and then exhales together. Everyone pauses before the talking piece is passed to the next person in the circle.

There are many different variations on the share circle. Some refer to it as circle work or council. Each community has its own rules for holding a space for conscious communication. The guidelines I have used for the many years come from the book *The Way of Council* by Jack Zimmerman and Virginia Coyle, whose approach to council practice coalesced at the Ojai Foundation in Ojai, California.

These are the four guidelines for council practice:

1. **Speak from the heart.** Move out of your head and mind. Settle into the space of your heart. Let your words come from this part of your body.

2. **Listen from the heart.** We are not in council practice to offer advice, psychoanalyze, judge, or fix each other. We are here to listen with compassion. Rather than listening from your mind, invite your listening to come down to the heart center. Make a practice of listening with kindness and empathy.

3. **Be spontaneous.** Try not to prepare your remarks while others are speaking from the heart. When the talking stick comes to you, simply say what is in your heart as you practice being in the present moment.

4. **Be of lean expression.** Get to the heart of what is
   in your heart. Don't say words just to say words.
   Be efficient and potent with your speech.

Often when I lead a share circle, in the first round I invite everyone to share their name, where they are from, and what called them to be here today. In round two, I may invite them to share what is in their heart or hasn't yet been spoken.

If you have enough time and the group seems up for it you can always go around again with a different invitation. If you are pressed for time, you can try the popcorn technique, where you place the talking piece in the center of the circle and allow anyone who feels like sharing to come into the circle and take the talking piece back to their seat for their share. When they are done, they simply place the piece back into the middle of the circle. This allows those who want to share to take the opportunity and those who are content to listen simply to sit back.

Here are a few examples of invitations to initiate group sharing:

- Tell us about your day. What did you notice?

- How are you feeling in your heart?

- What do you need today?

- What do you feel called to share with this group today?

- In what ways are you learning and growing?

Council practice builds community, strengthens the ability to listen deeply, and expands the practice of speaking from our hearts. In my experience, there is no other tool as effective for bringing together a group of people in a short amount of time. And when we practice council in a small group after a period of rewilding, we receive the gift of the community's shared wisdom on top of our individual experience.

Closing a Rewilding Experience

When it is time to leave the embrace of the living earth, you may have responsibilities to get back to, kids to pick up from school, or any number of other things that call you back to the modern world. Now, then, is a good time to acknowledge what you have received from your time outside. You may have tangible gifts, wonders you have gathered in gratitude from the abundance of the land, as well as the inner gifts, a feeling of peace, contentment, and perhaps connection and fellowship with the more-than-human world. Now is also the time to offer something back to the land, such as a silent prayer, spoken words of thanks, or an offering. You may place a stone or a flower on the earth or create a small design out of found objects. Whichever form of thanksgiving you choose, let it come from the heart. This expression of reciprocity with the land helps to strengthen your bond with a place that you are now drawing closer to.

In your rewilding journey, you will begin to feel that the more-than-human world of trees, stones, wind, and all the breathing, soaring, swimming, and crawling relatives is no longer a foreign world where you are a stranger. It will become your home away from home, a place where you belong. When you start having this experience, a new world has opened, one in which your isolation as a modern human has given way to your birthright as a human being at home on this earth.

Mindful rewilding supports a process of healing between the human species and the rest of the earth. As we draw closer to the mothering power of our planet, we show others that this path is available to them as well. We need not live as exiles. We can come home to the earth, and in so doing, to our true selves.

ACKNOWLEDGMENTS

I would like to gratefully acknowledge the support of my editor Leslie Meredith, Jaime Schwalb, and all the folks at Sounds True. I would also like to thank my advisors at Goddard who helped me open my mind to other perspectives on the topic of human rewilding. Sara, Caryn, Jim, and Lori—you guys have been such wise, kind, and powerful mentors. I am grateful for you.

A deep bow of appreciation to all of the teachers and depth practitioners within the Kripalu Yoga tradition, especially Kaviraj, Stephen Cope, and Yoganand Michael Carrol, who have kept the flame lit in their own unique ways all these years and passed on so much with kindness and care.

Special thanks to Grandfather and Tom Brown Jr., as well as the staff and teachers at the Tracker School, where I learned many of the hard and soft skills of nature connection, survival, and awareness. And to my friend and fellow mindful outdoor guide Mark Roule. Mark, thank you for blazing this new trail with me and sharing your wisdom and knowledge. I am grateful for your fellowship and support.

Also special thanks to my true soul friends and guides on this path: Tim Carlson, Brendan McKeever, Pete Schackner, Shaun Laframboise, Carl Hewitt, Walking Fox, Four Winds, and Ramtha. Thank you for standing as friends, guides, and great teachers along the way.

And finally, to the love of my life. Elaina, thank you for standing by my side and supporting me in the writing of this book and all I've taken on these past few years. Your support made all the difference. I love you always. You are my "density."

NOTES

Introduction

1. Jacqueline Howard, "Americans Devote More Than 10 Hours a Day to Screen Time, and Growing," *CNN*, July 29, 2016, cnn.com/2016/06/30/health/americans-screen-time-nielsen /index.html. Also, "The Inside Story: A Guide to Indoor Air Quality," accessed April 24, 2019, epa.gov/indoor-air-quality-iaq /inside-story-guide-indoor-air-quality.

Chapter 1: Mindful Rewilding

1. George Monbiot, *Feral: Rewilding the Land, the Sea, and Human Life* (Chicago: University of Chicago Press, 2014).
2. Thomas Berry, *The Great Work Our Way into the Future* (New York: Broadway Books, 2000), 32.
3. George Monbiot, *Feral*.
4. Robin Wall Kimmerer, *Braiding Sweetgrass: Indigenous Wisdom, Scientific Knowledge, and the Teachings of Plants* (Minneapolis: Milkweed Editions, 2015).
5. Edward O. Wilson, *Biophilia* (Cambridge, MA: Harvard University Press, 1984).
6. George Monbiot, *Feral*.
7. Luther Standing Bear, *My People the Sioux* (New York: Houghton Mifflin, 1928).
8. James Suzman, *Affluence Without Abundance: The Disappearing World of the Bushmen* (New York: Bloomsbury, 2017).
9. James Suzman, *Affluence Without Abundance*.
10. Adrienne A. Taren, et al., "Dispositional Mindfulness Co-Varies with Smaller Amygdala and Caudate Volumes in Community Adults," *PLOS ONE* 8, no. 5 (May 2013), journals.plos.org/plosone /article?id=10.1371/journal.pone.0064574.

Chapter 2: Eyes of the Eagle

1. Jules Evans, *Philosophy for Life and Other Dangerous Situations: Ancient Philosophy for Modern Problems* (Novato, CA: New World Library, 2013).
2. Frank White, *The Overview Effect: Space Exploration and Human Evolution* (Reston, VA: American Institute of Aeronautics and Astronautics, 2014).
3. Carl Sagan, *Pale Blue Dot: A Vision of the Human Future in Space* (New York: Ballantine Books, 1997).
4. "Penn Psychologists Study Intense Awe Astronauts Feel Viewing Earth from Space," Penn Today, accessed April 24, 2019, penntoday .upenn.edu/news/penn-psychologists-study-intense-awe-astronauts -feel-viewing-earth-space.
5. Joseph Campbell and Bill Moyers, *The Power of Myth* (New York: Anchor Books, 1991).
6. Thich Nhat Hanh, *The Miracle of Mindfulness: An Introduction to the Practice of Meditation* (New York: Beacon Press, 1999).
7. Thich Nhat Hanh, *The Miracle of Mindfulness.*
8. Mukunda Stiles, *Yoga Sutras of Patanjali: With Great Respect and Love* (Newburyport: Weiser Books, 2001).
9. Thich Nhat Hanh, *The Miracle of Mindfulness.*
10. Thich Nhat Hanh, *The Heart of the Buddha's Teaching: Transforming Suffering into Peace, Joy, and Liberation* (New York: Broadway Books, 1999).
11. Robin Wall Kimmerer, *Braiding Sweetgrass.*
12. Kamla K. Kapur, *Ganesha Goes to Lunch: Classics from Mystic India* (San Rafael: Mandala Publishing, 2007).

Chapter 3: The Living Earth

1. Brian Swimme, *The Universe Story: From the Primordial Flaring Forth to the Ecozoic Era—A Celebration of the Unfolding of the Cosmos* (New York: HarperOne, 1994).
2. Luther Standing Bear, *My People the Sioux.*
3. Peter Wohlleben, *The Hidden Life of Trees: What They Feel, How They Communicate—Discoveries from a Secret World* (Vancouver: Greystone Books, 2016).

4. "Facts & Statistics," Anxiety and Depression Association of America, accessed April 24, 2019, adaa.org/about-adaa/press-room /facts-statistics.
5. David Abram, *Becoming Animal: An Earthly Cosmology* (New York: Vintage, 2011).
6. Richard Louv, *The Nature Principle: Reconnecting with Life in a Virtual Age* (Chapel Hill: Algonquin Books, 2012).
7. Florence Williams, *The Nature Fix: Why Nature Makes Us Happier, Healthier, and More Creative* (New York: W. W. Norton & Company, 2018).
8. Florence Williams, *The Nature Fix*.
9. Florence Williams, *The Nature Fix*.
10. "World's Population Increasingly Urban with More Than Half Living in Urban Area," UN, accessed April 24, 2019, un.org/en /development/desa/news/population/world-urbanization -prospects-2014.html.
11. "Noncommunicable Diseases," World Health Organization, accessed April 24, 2019, who.int/news-room/fact-sheets/detail /noncommunicable-diseases.

Chapter 4: Reclaiming Skills

1. Edward O. Wilson, *The Social Conquest of Earth* (New York: Liveright, 2013).
2. David Brewster, *Memoirs of the Life, Writings, and Discoveries of Sir Isaac Newton: Volume 2* (Boston: Adamant Media Corporation, 2001).

Chapter 6: Putting It All Together

1. Tom Brown Jr., *Tom Brown's Field Guide to Nature and Survival for Children* (New York: Berkley, 1989).

RESOURCES

If you are interested in continuing your rewilding journey, here are some resources you may find helpful.

1. Association of Nature and Forest Therapy (ANFT) was founded by Amos Clifford, the foremost forest-bathing teacher in North America. Amos has helped to bring forest therapy from Japan to the West, and he has a wonderful book called *Your Guide to Forest Bathing*, which is a terrific resource for anyone interested in the practice. You can also train to become a forest-bathing guide with ANFT. You will find them at natureandforesttherapy.org.

2. The Kripalu School of Mindful Outdoor Leadership (KSMOL) is part of the Kripalu Center for Yoga & Health in the Berkshires of western Massachusetts. KSMOL offers training and practice in mindfulness, forest bathing, yoga, Ayurveda, and naturalist and ancestral skills, which lead to certification as a mindful outdoor guide. Mindful outdoor guides go on to lead their communities to deeper connection with their lands and themselves. You can learn more at kripalu.org /schools/kripalu-school-mindful-outdoor-leadership.

3. The *Rewild Yourself* podcast with Daniel Vitalis is a deep dive into all things rewilding. Informative and insightful interviews on a variety of rewilding topics with experts in the field make this podcast an excellent resource.

4. The Tracker School in the Pine Barrens of New Jersey is taught by Tom Brown Jr. and his highly trained staff. This is a place to learn tracking and earth-based survival skills from the best. Tom is a renowned tracker and rewilding expert in North America. His books and trainings have cleared the way for much of the other rewilding work that is happening today. You can learn more at trackerschool.com.

5. The Wilderness Awareness School (WAS) was created by bird language expert Jon Young, a former student of Tom Brown Jr. WAS teaches a variety of topics related to rewilding and strengthening our connection with nature. Jon Young's books *What the Robin Knows* and *Coyote's Guide* are also loaded with useful and inspiring information about drawing closer to the earth. To learn more, go to wildernessawareness.org.

BIBLIOGRAPHY

Abram, David. *Becoming Animal: An Earthly Cosmology*. New York: Vintage, 2011.

Abram, David. *The Spell of the Sensuous: Perception and Language in a More-Than-Human World*. New York: Vintage, 1997.

Berry, Thomas. *The Great Work: Our Way into the Future*. New York: Broadway Books, 2000.

Bowman, Katy. *Move Your DNA: Restore Your Health Through Natural Movement*. Sequim, WA: Propriometrics Press, 2014.

Brewster, David. *Memoirs of the Life, Writings, and Discoveries of Sir Isaac Newton: Volume 2*. Boston: Adamant Media Corporation, 2001.

Brown, Joseph Epes. *Animals of the Soul: Sacred Animals of the Oglala Sioux*. Rockport, MA: Element Books, Ltd., 1992.

Brown, Tom, Jr. *Tom Brown's Field Guide to Nature and Survival for Children*. New York: Berkley, 1989.

Brown, Tom, Jr. *Tom Brown's Science and Art of Tracking: Nature's Path to Spiritual Discovery*. New York: Berkley, 1999.

Campbell, Joseph, and Bill Moyers. *The Power of Myth*. New York: Anchor Books, 1991.

Chi, Tom. "Everything Is Connected—Here's How." YouTube. Accessed April 24, 2019. https://www.youtube.com/watch?v=zyr4qORDu2A.

Easwaran, Eknath. *The Bhagavad Gita for Daily Living*. Mumbai: Jaico, 2009.

Easwaran, Eknath. *The Upanishads*. Tomales, CA: Nilgiri Press, 2007.

Evans, Jules. *Philosophy for Life and Other Dangerous Situations: Ancient Philosophy for Modern Problems*. Novato, CA: New World Library, 2013.

Gollner, Adam. *The Book of Immortality: The Science, Belief, and Magic Behind Living Forever*. New York: Scribner, 2013.

Hanh, Thich Nhat. *The Pocket Thich Nhat Hanh*. Edited by Melvin McLeod. Boulder, CO: Shambhala Pocket Classics, 2012.

Hanh, Thich Nhat, Vo-Dinh Mai, and Mobi Ho. *The Miracle of Mindfulness: An Introduction to the Practice of Meditation*. New York: Beacon Press, 1999.

Kimmerer, Robin Wall. *Braiding Sweetgrass: Indigenous Wisdom, Scientific Knowledge, and the Teachings of Plants*. Minneapolis: Milkweed Editions, 2015.

Leopold, Aldo. *A Sand County Almanac: Outdoor Essays and Reflections*. New York: Ballantine Books, 1986.

Louv, Richard. *Last Child in the Woods: Saving Our Children from Nature-Deficit Disorder*. Chapel Hill: Algonquin Books, 2008.

Louv, Richard. *The Nature Principle: Reconnecting with Life in a Virtual Age*. Chapel Hill: Algonquin Books, 2012.

McKibben, Bill. *The Age of Missing Information*. New York: Random House Trade Paperbacks, 2006.

Monbiot, George. *Feral: Rewilding the Land, the Sea, and Human Life*. Chicago: University of Chicago Press, 2014.

Muir, John. *John of the Mountains: The Unpublished Journals of John Muir*. Edited by Linnie Marsh Wolfe. Madison: University of Wisconsin Press, 1979.

Neihardt, John, and Nicholas Black Elk. *Black Elk Speaks: Being the Life Story of a Holy Man of the Oglala Sioux*. Lincoln: University of Nebraska Press, 2005.

New American Standard Bible. Carol Stream: Creation House. Several editions since 1971.

Prabhavananda, Swami, and Christopher Ishwerwood, trans. *Bhagavad-Gita: The Song of God*. New York: Signet, 2002.

Pyle, Robert Michael. *Thunder Tree: Lessons from an Urban Wildland*. Corvallis: Oregon State University Press, 2011.

Schaefer, Carol. *Grandmothers Counsel the World: Women Elders Offer Their Vision for Our Planet.* New York: Trumpeter, 2006.

Selhub, Eva M., and Alan C. Logan. *Your Brain on Nature: The Science of Nature's Influence on Your Health, Happiness, and Vitality.* New York: Collins, 2014.

Standing Bear, Luther. *My People the Sioux.* New York: Houghton Mifflin. 1928.

Stevenson, Robert Louis. *The Complete Works of Robert Louis Stevenson: Novels, Short Stories, Poems, Plays, Memoirs, Travel Sketches, Letters and Essays (Illustrated Edition).* E-art now, 2015.

Stiles, Mukunda. *Yoga Sutras of Patanjali: With Great Respect and Love.* Newburyport, MA: Weiser Books, 2001.

Suzman, James. *Affluence Without Abundance: The Disappearing World of the Bushmen.* New York: Bloomsbury, 2017.

Tibbitts, Clark. *Aging in the Modern World: Selections from the Literature of Aging for Pleasure and Instruction.* Ann Arbor: University of Michigan, 1957.

Tzu, Lao, and Stephen Mitchell. *Tao Te Ching: A New English Version.* New York: Harper Perennial Modern Classics, 2006.

Vasu, Rai Bahadur Srisa Chandra. *The Siva Samhita.* New Delhi: Munshiram, 1996.

White, Frank. *The Overview Effect: Space Exploration and Human Evolution.* Reston, VA: American Institute of Aeronautics and Astronautics, 2014.

Williams, Florence. *The Nature Fix: Why Nature Makes Us Happier, Healthier, and More Creative.* New York: W. W. Norton & Company, 2018.

Wilson, Edward O. *Biophilia.* Cambridge, MA: Harvard University Press, 1984.

Wilson, Edward O. *The Social Conquest of Earth.* New York: Liveright, 2013.

Young, Jon. *What the Robin Knows: How Birds Reveal the Secrets of the Natural World.* New York: Mariner Books, 2013.

Zimmerman, Jack, and Virginia Coyle. *The Way of Council.* Putney, VT: Bramble Books, 2009.

INDEX

ABOUT THE AUTHOR

Micah Mortali is the director of the Kripalu Schools, which includes the School of Yoga, Ayurveda, Integrative Yoga Therapy, and the School of Mindful Outdoor Leadership (which he founded in 2018).

Micah holds a master's degree in health arts and sciences from Goddard College and leads trainings and retreats year-round.

Micah is a Level 2 Mindful Outdoor Guide, a 500-hour Kripalu Yoga teacher, and an ancestral-skills and mindful-rewilding enthusiast, with a passion for bridging the world of meditation with the world of the outdoors. He has been leading groups in wilderness and retreat settings for almost twenty years.

Micah lives in Pittsfield, Massachusetts, with his wife and children, where he enjoys nothing more than a good outdoor fire in any season with friends and family.

ABOUT SOUNDS TRUE

Sounds True is a multimedia publisher whose mission is to inspire and support personal transformation and spiritual awakening. Founded in 1985 and located in Boulder, Colorado, we work with many of the leading spiritual teachers, thinkers, healers, and visionary artists of our time. We strive with every title to preserve the essential "living wisdom" of the author or artist. It is our goal to create products that not only provide information to a reader or listener, but that also embody the quality of a wisdom transmission.

For those seeking genuine transformation, Sounds True is your trusted partner. At SoundsTrue.com you will find a wealth of free resources to support your journey, including exclusive weekly audio interviews, free downloads, interactive learning tools, and other special savings on all our titles.

To learn more, please visit SoundsTrue.com/freegifts or call us toll-free at 800.333.9185.

sounds true
WAKING UP THE WORLD